Pilgrims of a Common Life

Pilgrims of a Common Life

*Christian Community of Goods
Through the Centuries*

Trevor J. Saxby

Foreword by Donald F. Durnbaugh

HERALD PRESS
Scottdale, Pennsylvania
Kitchener, Ontario
1987

Library of Congress Cataloging-in-Publication Data
Saxby, Trevor, J. (Trevor John), 1954-
  Pilgrims of a common life.

  Bibliography: p.
  Includes indexes.
  1. Christian communities.   2. Property—Religious
aspects—Christianity.   3. Poverty (Virtue)   I. Title.
BV4405.S24   1987   262   86-27043
ISBN 0-8361-3426-5

The cover photo was taken inside the Feast Hall at the Old
Economy Village near Pittsburgh, Pennsylvania, the final loca-
tion of the community founded by George Rapp. Since 1917,
the Pennsylvania (State) Historical and Museum Commission
has been steward of the physical remnants of the communitarian group, "The Harmony Society." See page 138ff. Photo
copyright © 1986 by David Hiebert.

Unless otherwise indicated, Scripture references are taken from
the Revised Standard Version of the Bible, copyrighted 1946,
1952, © 1971, 1973.

PILGRIMS OF A COMMON LIFE
Copyright © 1987 by Herald Press, Scottdale, Pa. 15683
  Published simultaneously in Canada by Herald Press,
  Kitchener, Ont. N2G 4M5. All rights reserved
Library of Congress Catalog Card Number: 86-27043
International Standard Book Number: 0-8361-3426-5
Printed in the United States of America
Design by David Hiebert

92 91 90 89 88 87 10 9 8 7 6 5 4 3 2 1

To my brothers and sisters of the New Creation Christian Community
from whom I learn so much.

Contents

Foreword

In an orderly and logical progression, Trevor J. Saxby has introduced the recurring phenomenon of Christian communalism, discussed its scriptural foundations, narrated the historical development by centuries, and then summarized the characteristics of Christian community. Of necessity, these subjects are described in rather brief, overview fashion, but the reader does not have the feeling of sketchiness. Rather, there is the impression of well-considered conciseness and briskness, without unwarranted detail. Even so, the specialist may well learn here of movements previously unknown and gain new insights.

The increasing number of Christians challenged by the Anabaptist vision of discipleship will find in this book a thoughtful, biblically based, and historically sound portrayal of Christian communitarianism. Not all will follow the author in concluding that this form of social arrangement is the preferred form. But all will need to take seriously the evidence for its appropriateness contained in this treatise.

The author frankly sets forth his dual aim: "to record and preserve the history of a biblical teaching and tradition" *and* "to advocate a vision for contemporary discipleship." *Pilgrims of a Common Life*, therefore, is not a dispassionate and coldly scientific study. It is history written for a purpose, seeking a response in the reader.

That is not to say that it avoids facing squarely the problems which have arisen in Christian communities. These dilemmas are fairly portrayed. The reader is fairly forewarned, however, that the book was written out of a positive, even compelling conviction of the rightness of Christian communal association.

Sociologists such as Robert Bellah and his colleagues in the

book *Habits of the Heart* (1985) tell us that modern Western
society suffers from a rampant individualism that sees personal
self-interest and pleasure as the only benchmarks. Although in
earlier years the utilitarian ethic was understood as that which
brought the most good to the most people, it has now taken on a
selfish bent as a utilitarianism of private interest. "The right act
is simply the one that yields the agent the most exciting
challenge or the most good feeling about himself. . . . In the
absence of any objectifiable criteria of right and wrong, good or
evil, the self and its feelings become our only moral guide" (p.
76). Indeed, it is not difficult to find a great deal of evidence for
this judgment as one surveys the passing scene.

But at the same time, there is a countervailing movement—
perhaps in reaction to the crass and unlovely individualism of
the age. This is the revival of Christian communalism. Increasing numbers of Christians, including highly educated
professionals, are finding renewed faith and strength in some
form of communal living. In the 1960s many communes were
connected with the so-called Jesus movement. Many others
were characterized as countercultural and identified with the
hippie generation. Journalistic estimates reached the ten thousand mark for urban and rural communes in the USA alone. In
fact, no one knew the true extent of the phenomenon.

In quieter, less publicized ways, a large number of Christian
communitarians have gathered in a variety of cultures. Their
aim has been simple obedience to Jesus Christ and mutual support in their Christian pilgrimage. The present book arises from
one of the more important of these developments in England.
The author has sought to place his own spiritual walk, which
brought him into community, within the larger Christian story.

Another Englishman, the noted Roman Catholic and biblical
translator R. A. Knox, wrote a somewhat similar book in 1950
entitled *Enthusiasm: A Chapter in the History of Religion.* Although covering many of the same movements, the book by
Knox was dedicated to the vindication of the Mother Church

and to the defeat of the "heresies." Interestingly, however, despite his conviction of its superior worth and spirituality, his final words were of the limits inherent in the institutional church: "But there is danger in her position none the less; where wealth abounds, it is easy to mistake shadow for substance; the fires of spirituality may burn low, and we go on unconscious, dazzled by the glare of tinsel suns. How nearly we thought we could do without St. Francis, without St. Ignatius! Men will not live without vision; that moral we do well to carry away with us from contemplating in so many strange forms, the record of the visionaries" (pp. 590-591).

Those Christians who are comfortable in their institutional churches will do well to listen to the testimonies brought together here in *Pilgrims of a Common Life*. The communitarian witness is needed to enrich the common pilgrimage.

—Donald F. Durnbaugh
Bethany Theological Seminary
Oak Brook, Illinois 60521

Author's Preface

I well remember my own path to community living: the awkward smiles of Christian friends whenever I mentioned the idea; the paternal concern of my well-read pastor as he assured me it was all a novelty with little historical foundation; the distress of my relatives (happily soon cured) at the thought of me, as they saw it, being sucked into a cult; and all the time the inner urge that would not leave me alone, telling me that it *was* God's will for today.

So the research for this volume began out of personal interest and was given direction by my own community, which encouraged me to discover something of our communitarian roots. The path has been long and at times tortuous, but the view has always been exhilarating.

On entering the only partly charted realm of communitarian history, I constantly experienced the danger of losing my way in the complexities of varied interpretations. I chose therefore to limit myself to those communities where some form of community of goods was recognized practice.

Even so, pitfalls remained, for what was I to make of communistic groups that would certainly have called themselves Christian but which held heterodox, or even heretical, beliefs: Oneida, the Shakers, the early Mormons? I found in the end that they had to be omitted, simply because the sidetrack could prove endless. After all, Christian communities are often suspected of enough novelty and bad hermeneutics, without adding the "lunatic fringe."

My final obstacle towered above me as I began to process my material. What was my aim: to record and preserve the history of a biblical teaching and tradition, or to advocate a vision for contemporary discipleship? I must honestly answer, both. I was keen to help others avoid my own frustration at finding so little in print on the continuance of a practice as old as the church itself. The few writers to attempt such an overview merely referred to each other and said little that was new.

So objectivity was *de rigueur*, the straight facts, including the warts. And yet I could not altogether deny my positive stance on the subject and my conviction that all Christians ought to look fairly and squarely at the common life of sharing as an alternative to materialism and greed, and if therefore such a bias has intruded at times, despite my careful editing, the reader will, I hope, excuse me.

I gladly acknowledge the help and advice of Prof. Giovanni Gonnet of the University of Rome, Dr. Peter Biller of the University of York, and Janet Halton, archivist at Moravian Church House, London. My thanks also to Prof. "Jack" McManners, of All Souls College, Oxford, who read several chapters and aided me with his astute comments. Not least am I indebted to my wife and my brothers and sisters of the New Creation Christian Community (Jesus Fellowship Church, Baptist), who have encouraged me and borne with my biblio-mania throughout this research. One, Rifka Pickering, nobly typed the manuscript.

—Cornhill Manor, Pattishall
Northamptonshire

Pilgrims of a Common Life

Chapter 1
The Vision and the Obstacles

To approach the subject of Christian community in our day is to plunge straight into confusion. The problem is not, however, entirely of our own making. Central to it all is the sheer diversity of applications contained in the word *community*, covering as it does so many facets of religious and social life. The Greek philosophers basically defined community as the relation of the individual to those around him or her—a very broad denominator! Yet even here they disagreed. Some believed that a common *goal* was enough to constitute a community. Others felt such a grouping would need a definite *form* and structure to merit the term.

There was, however, basic agreement that people relate communally in two areas: *politeia*, the public life of a person's city or republic, and *oikonomia*, a person's household life. Add to this the religious aspect of life, with worshipers united in devotion at the shrine, and community is straightway seen to have political, social, and religious interpretations.

The advent of Christianity immediately brought the issue into stark focus, for here was what early church writers called "a third race," "a peculiar people"—a people who had been told by their Lord that they were to be *in* the world but not *of* it.[1] John strongly condemned the world *(kosmos)* as being under the power of Satan. It was not to be loved by those who follow Christ.[2] This shows that Jesus' message swept away the existing notions of *politeia* and *oikonomia* as the true basis of man's relatings and set up a new social order based on separation from the old. After all, Jesus had said that his kingdom was not of the world and that his followers had been given to him *out* of it. They were to continue living in the world but were not to consider themselves as any longer belonging to it.[3]

The message was clear: an alternative society operating within the wider social context—a community within a community, demonstrating to the larger organism that its whole foundation for living was wrong. Paul's words in Ephesians 2:19 sum up the process: "You are no longer strangers and sojourners, but you are fellow citizens with the saints and members of the household of God." Here is the language of the old order: "citizens"—the *politeia* and "household"—the *oikonomia*. Both are entirely reconstituted in Christ. The average convert had lived "in community" by the accepted norms, but in God's terms had still been a wayfarer without a true home. Now, through Christ, he entered a *new* "polis," a *new* "oikos": the church of God.

However, as a subsequent chapter will show, the issue became blurred once more in the fourth century when the emperor Constantine, for reasons largely political, made Christianity the accepted faith of the empire. The inevitable consequence was that the radical, separated social body of the church became enmeshed once more in the world's system. The empire became "sacral,"[4] with religion and politics as inseparable partners. Every member of society automatically assumed that society's religion and its demands.

For the true church, this now meant an unquestioning surrender to whatever the state-church authorities decreed. The very idea would have horrified the first apostles, for the very *kosmos* which they had so opposed was now back in control. The wider community was now a "Christian" (or at least Christianized) community, divided into parishes which were at the same time pastoral and political units, and administered by priest and magistrate operating as equals.

The Terminology

The legacy of such a fusion is still with us. In some European languages there is one word to cover both "church congregation" and "local community": German, *Gemeinde;* Dutch, *gemeente.* French does nearly the same with *commune,* and English with *community.* Taken in its social sense, *everybody* lives in community, unless perhaps they are vagrants or recluses. This has colored the Christian interpretation of the word, for being "in community" has meant anything from inner-city social work to running the parish rummage sale.[5]

Sociologists have sought to reach some definition of what constitutes community, and each interpretation has something of interest to the Christian. Ferdinand Tönnies distinguished between "society," which he saw in larger towns, and "community," which was confined to rural areas.[6] Since then, various propositions have been made: a loose-knit collection of human beings; an identifiable territory or locality, be it village or inner-city area; a group of people linked by shared activities; or a kinship of social relationship, predominantly within extended families. Was the heart of community what it *was* or what its members *felt:* a sense of solidarity, fulfillment, identity?[7] A glance at a reputable dictionary suffices to show how varied the interpretations of "community" can be.

Yet it is significant to note that the first listed meaning is *joint ownership.* The Christian will immediately think of the Pentecostal community at Jerusalem, where possessions were shared in common out of love for Christ. To put together the various strands and attempt some working definition, we are left with the following consensus: *an organized religious or social body with distinct identity of creed and character, living in one locality in fellowship together and* (for Christians) *sharing material blessings in common.*

In early English another term gained popularity that also deserves consideration: *commonwealth,* derived, not from "common wealth" as one might suppose, but "common weal" (i.e., common good). This was a term popular among those determined enough to plow through the *Summa Theologica* of Thomas Aquinas, who repeatedly taught that God wills to draw humanity into "the community of his enjoyment." People are created in such a way that they find true fulfillment only as they devote that knowledge of God to the *common good*. Aquinas interpreted this as involving a true bond of Christian brotherhood in a life of community, which is alone the basis for individual and social stability.

Interpreted thus, the term *community* is not as vague. It includes the notion of a voluntary surrender of individual ends in favor of mutual benefit and support, which is the only possible outworking of the scriptural injunctions to love one another and not look to one's own good (e.g., see Phil. 2:4 and 1 John 4:7).

Jesus' Example

The Lord himself provided the model for the "all in common" life, for whatever he had, be it time, abilities, teaching, compassion, or strength, he lavished on others and did not keep it to himself. As for finances, we know that he and the twelve held a common purse, entrusted to Judas Iscariot, and that this supply was sometimes supplemented by donations from others.[8] He proved that the new life which he brought was to be expressed in a new lifestyle, motivated by love. Our heart having been renewed, our living was to speak of unity, justice, honesty, and brotherly affection. It was to bear testimony to Jesus himself. Both went together, both were God's will, both were the good news.

Nowadays the impression is easily given in Christian circles that only the first part was good news (a personal relationship with Jesus which is largely a hidden matter), while the second part was really rather bad news. For it is cozy and flattering to our human selfishness to hear of love, forgiveness, peace, and the like, but nature rebels against what it sees as overdemanding, restrictive, and extreme in such matters as poverty (Luke 12:33), forsaking all things to be a disciple (Luke 14:33; 5:11), persecution and rejection (John 15:20), and living from a common purse (John 13:29). Yet the two are inseparable, and the Lord who stressed that we must be *doers* of the word, meant it that way.

The Example of the Early Church

The Pentecostal Jerusalem church was moved by the Holy Spirit in precisely such a way. The Spirit filled each heart with divine love and power which then found its natural outworking in the sharing of possessions, so that all who were now united and equal in the blessings of God might also be so in temporal things:

> Now the company of those who believed were of one heart and soul, and no one said that any of the things which he possessed was his own, but they had everything in common. And with great power the apostles gave their testimony to the resurrection of the Lord Jesus, and great grace was upon them all. There was not a needy person among them, for as many as were possessors of lands or houses sold them, and brought the proceeds of what was sold and laid it at the apostles' feet; and distribution was made to each as any had need (Acts 4:32-35).

The facts are clear-cut and conclusive. Yet within twenty years there was a change. The Jerusalem community continued in communal sharing, the pooled goods and income stewarded by deacons, but the believers scattered by the persecutions of Saul of Tarsus (Acts 9) and Herod Agrippa (Acts 12) spread far and wide, encountering new cultures and Gentile rulers. We are nowhere definitely told that they continued to share all things. Many have therefore looked back on the communal sharing at Jerusalem as an experiment. And once they find later evidence of believers allowed to keep their possessions and give alms, they conclude with relief that community living finished with Jerusalem and was practiced nowhere else.

Attempts to Define "Communal Sharing"

The question of Christian community—so pure, so simple, so joyful at its inception—has been clouded ever since. Theologians and church groups have adopted stances at various points between two extremes: one that full communal sharing is an obligation, the other that it was a huge mistake. The usual position is to admire the Jerusalem saints for what they did, to acknowledge that some form of justice and sharing is probably right, and to point to the fact that, in all ages since, the development of sharing communities has been peripheral to the mainstream development of the church. These are then regarded as sufficient grounds for sweeping the whole matter conveniently under the carpet.

Other issues have clouded the matter still further. In the ensuing centuries there have been any number of splinter groups which have shared all things in common while indulging in other practices that are far from commendable. Examples of this include the messianic kingdom at Münster, with a peasant crowned as king and wives held in common; the breakaway Franciscans under Fra Dolcino (who had himself wrapped in swaddling clothes and laid in a manger); the Doukhobors, who have been known to strip naked or to set fire to their own houses under supposed inspiration; and any number of millenarian sects who have huddled on hilltops or islands expecting the second coming within the next few days. All have led the common person to reject communal sharing along with the aberrations as just one symptom of fanaticism.

Since the beginning of monasticism, most groups that have shared all things in common have also seceded from the established church: Protestant groups from Rome, various independent sects from Protestantism. Therefore, each group is distinctive and needs to be approached in its own right. Each has found itself with a name it would not have chosen. Normally the name is based on that of the founder or leader of the group in question. So while these communitarian churches usually styled themselves "brethren" or "Christians," history has filed them away as '-ists' and 'ites': Donatists, Labadists, Hutterites, Mennonites, Rappites, and many others. The biggest disadvantage of this is its suggestion that the center of the community was not God or fraternal love, but a man, and probably a misguided man at that.

The problem has come to the forefront particularly at the present time (i.e., since the mid-1970s) with the rise of the religious cults. In an age where dissatisfaction with materialism and the impersonal nature of society are causing young people to look for alternatives, the extremist cults have grown and blossomed. Gurus and "prophets" in plenty have drawn many people by their supposed depth of spirituality and by the strength of commitment binding their followers. The cult answers the need for individual and corporate identity. It usually provides for its members, and in many cases sobers up those who were formerly wild and dissolute.

Several of the cults share what they have. The false teachings, dangerous ascetic practices, and occult dabblings easily prove that they are misguided, but the cults do practice things which Jesus enjoined on his own followers, such as self-denial, sacrificial giving, and separation from the world. As such they form a subtle blend of good and evil, light and darkness, and have done true Christianity great harm by casting a shadow on the more radical aspects of discipleship. Even the very love which is the highest command and fruit of all has been debased. Some modern sects have even embraced cult prostitution. As a result, any orthodox Christians seeking to love one another and share in community run the risk of being mistaken for a cult, their efforts derided and opposed.

Heresy and Nonconformity

But what is *heresy?* The term *heresy* comes from a Greek word implying "to choose between various options." A heretic was one who had drifted away from "the sure word as taught" (2 Thess. 2:15; Titus 1:9) and chosen a doctrine which did not accord with Scripture. From earliest times the church came under subtle attack from heresies, as Scripture had foretold (Acts 20:29-30). Pelagians, Arians, Marcionites, and many more rejected aspects of God's revealed Word and were excommunicated from the church.

But what happened if the church itself departed from the God-given norm? From the time of Emperor Constantine onward, many groups did indeed hold the established church to have fallen by embracing the world. They therefore sought to return to the apostolic pattern of exclusive gatherings of regenerate believers, separated from the world. Several of these churches practiced "all things in common." The established church, however, held the reins and was able to anathematize such groups as heretics for not having toed the line.

To make the charge stick, the name of a known heresy was usually added, the most convenient being that of Manichaeism. The Manichaeans attempted to account for the apparent discrepancy between the God of vengeance and the God of love by inventing a dualistic system: the vengeful God was of the old covenant and linked with the fallen earth, and he had now been supplanted by the loving God, whose rule was spiritual. Matter was therefore evil and only what was spiritual was of importance. Rome took this to be the motivation behind any group seeking to separate from the world and live a life of love in the Holy Spirit. Thus many a group was branded Manichaean, either in its day or retrospectively. Only the discovery of new source material in later years has proven the charge to be false, or at least open to dispute. Priscillian in the early Church and Henry of Lausanne in medieval times are just two examples of those whose reputation has, as it were, been cleared. Many a communitarian group, however, still lies under the anathema of heresy, with little or no genuine evidence for or against such a charge.

A final difficulty arises for any historian trying to trace the thin red line of "all things in common" throughout church history. Until the advent of printing and higher levels of literacy among poorer classes, it was costly and laborious to write books. Few could do it and not many read them once completed. Moreover, until the hold of Rome was loosened at the Reformation, the Inquisition had its ways of rounding up any literature which it suspected of novelty or danger, and burning it. Therefore it is often hard to know just where a particular early or medieval sect stood in doctrine and practice. If it was conjectured that the group was heretical, its records were seized. Often all that was left to posterity were accounts of its supposed errors written by its opponents—hardly an unbiased legacy! Any group preaching separation from the wicked generation of this world (Acts 2:40; 1 John 5:19) was considered guilty of the heretical dualism of the Manichaeans.

The Pilgrim Church

Such preconceptions have dogged the impartial study of such dissenting churches for centuries. What, though, could be less objectionable than the "Seven Ordinances of the True Church," penned by the Anabaptist, Dirck Philips, around 1560? This reflects the basic tenets of all separatist, "all-things-in-common" movements down the years:

1. True teaching and correct ministry.
2. Proper use of the two sacraments of baptism and communion.
3. Foot washing.
4. Separation from the spirit of the world.
5. Brotherly love, mutual admonition, communal sharing.
6. Keeping all the Lord's commandments.
7. Accepting suffering and persecution.

Radical reforming groups, whether sectarian or monastic, and the common living which they advocated were, it is true, largely on the fringes of the main development of the established church. Yet, together they form a pedigree as old, and indeed older, than that of the state-church. They constitute what the seventeenth-century Independent Comenius called "the seed of survival," or what E. H. Broadbent has more recently termed "the pilgrim church." Unlike its established stepmother, this church knows that it is not of this present world and its base spirit. It is rather a separate, regenerate entity which lives on earth the communal, devoted life of Paradise. This is the path which this study will attempt to trace, pitted though it is with the potholes already mentioned.

Pre-Christian Communalism

Before examining at any length the scriptural position regarding the common life and sharing of goods, we should note that such a notion did not originate with the Holy Spirit's descent at Jerusalem. The Greeks had invented the Golden Age, an ideal society in which injustice would be eradicated and all would live in harmony. Being only a concept and not a reality, suggestions varied as to how it ought to be run, but there was general agreement that the prime obstacle to such a system was the root of pride and avarice in the human heart. So there arose various figures and groups advocating a strict asceticism and, at least in measure, the sharing of material things.

In the 6th century B.C., Pythagoras is said to have urged the inhabitants of Magna Graecia to put all their goods into a common fund so that there be no rich and no poor; he also enforced community of goods upon any wishing to join his philosophical school (which had a five-year probationary period), with the provision that possessions could be returned if anyone chose to leave. In 580 Diodor reported a communistic settlement on the island of Lipara off Sicily. All land was held corporately by the inhabitants who had come from Rhodes and Cnidus and meals were eaten communally.

It was, however, the fifth century B.C. that saw the greatest development of communitarian notions. The protracted Peloponnesian war and the final demoralization of defeat by Sparta led the philosophers and writers of Athens to consider new social structures. Aristophanes' comedy *Women in Parliament*, though basically a caricature, presents the views of such a communitarian school of thought through this speech by the heroine, Praxagora:

> The rule which I dare to enact and declare
> Is that all should be equal and equally share
> All wealth and enjoyments, nor longer endure
> That one should be rich and another be poor. [10]

Others took the idea more seriously. Aristotle, in a discourse on friendship, [11] quotes the proverbs *koina ta philōn* ("between friends all things are in common") and *en koinonia ē philia* ("friendship is in sharing"). Elsewhere he refers to one Phaleas of Chalcedon, who advocated an equal redistribution of wealth.

Plato, in his *Republic*, concludes that the only truly moral and just society was one of full sharing: "They must have no private houses or land or any private possessions; they receive their upkeep from the other citizens, and they must spend it in common." [12] The fact that he went on to advocate community of wives merely highlights the flaws in an idealistic human attempt to work what is not really possible without the renewal of the heart by the Holy Spirit.

Such concepts continued through to New Testament times, though only as ideas and philosophies, with little done in practice. Aratus did not want fields divided up among individuals. Stoic and Cynic missionary-philosophers renounced all property and lived a life strikingly similar to that of the early mendicant friars. Virgil speaks of "the love of possessing" as a powerful force undermining social life. [13] The idealistic Age of Saturn, of which we read principally in Virgil and Ovid, [14] was to be based upon community of goods.

In some cases the theory went hand in hand with practice, and certain ascetic communities did exist in pre-Pentecost days. The Therapeutae of the first century B.C. were spread over a wide area of Egypt, especially around Alexandria and on the shores of Lake Marea. They fled cities and chose to live in unpopulated places, where they set up community villages, with individual dwellings grouped around a communal building. All members renounced their possessions at the time of joining and gave themselves to a contemplative life. Men and women could join, but strict celibacy was to be observed. The day was given over to prayer, meditation, and a single meal. Curiously enough, in contrast with later Christian communities, there was no manual work. A covenant bound them together and they had a period of waiting, similar to a novitiate, before any joined them. The early historian Philo of Alexandria, who knew the Therapeutae, wrote in A.D. 20 in praise of the simplicity and discipline of their way of life:

> The effort to gain a livelihood and make money breeds injustice through the inequality entailed, while the opposite principle of action begets justice through equality. . . . So when they have given up possession of their property . . . they spend their time pursuing solitude in gardens or solitary places.[15]

In the same period a new sect arose among the Jews, called the Essenes. Many of these chose to live communally, sharing goods and possessions, in the belief that such righteousness could in part atone for the degeneracy of Israel. In an Essene settlement, life centered around a communal building which served both as dining room and tabernacle. Families lived alone, but their homes were open at any hour to other Essenes, even those who chose not to live communally. Unlike the Therapeutae, the Essenes held to the goodness of labor and were skilled in crafts and agriculture. They tolerated marriage but advocated celibacy as a way of losing worldly cares and increasing devotion to God. Philo knew of the Essenes also and wrote of them:

> There is but one purse for them all and a common expenditure. Their clothes and food are also held in common, for they have adopted the practice of eating together. In vain would one search elsewhere for a more effective sharing of the same roof, the same way of life and the same table. This is the reason: nothing which they receive as salary for their day's work is kept to themselves, but is deposited before them all, in their midst, to be put to the common employment of those who wish to make use of it. [16]

The Jewish historian Josephus also knew the Essene communities:

> Their practice of righteousness is admirable ... they put their property into a common stock, and the rich man enjoys no more of his fortune than does the man with absolutely nothing. And there are more than 4,000 men who behave this way. [17]

And the Roman writer, Pliny the Elder, who died in the eruption of Vesuvius in A.D. 79, commented with some scorn: 'Owing to the throng of newcomers, this people is daily reborn ... indeed, those whom, wearied by the fluctuations of fortune, life leads to adopt their customs, stream in in great numbers.' [18]

The Essene communities lasted until the Romans sacked Jerusalem in A.D. 70. The same campaign also marked the end of another community (presumed to be Essene but not without dispute) at Qumran. Situated in the desert by the Dead Sea, it has achieved fame through the discovery of the Dead Sea Scrolls, which were part of its library, hidden to escape destruction by the Romans. Much speculation has surrounded the community at Qumran. Some suspect that Jesus knew it. Others think it more than likely that John the Baptist was linked to it.

From its writings much has been learned about life in the

community. It spoke of itself as "the community" and of its members as "the men of holiness." Its *Book of the Rule* states that they were to "eat in common, pray in common and deliberate in common," so that they might "practice truth in common, and humility, and righteousness, and justice and loving charity, and modesty in all their ways." The members were to share "understanding, powers and possessions" and live in strict obedience to the law of Moses. Because they saw the rest of Judaism as backslidden, they vowed to be separate from ungodly men and make atonement by prayer and devotions. They were to be truthful, humble, just, and loving, bound together in what they termed "the community of the eternal covenant."[19]

The looser adherents were allowed to dwell nearer to the towns and practice a less demanding rule. They joined their brethren in the desert annually to celebrate the feast of the Renewal of the Covenant. The stricter members held firmly to the notion of the "faithful remnant in the land" and bound themselves together by a strict covenant (after a probationary period of upwards of two years), during which time they were regularly examined by the Superior. Once received, they devoted themselves to prayer and to labor: farming, pottery, leather-curing, and reproduction of manuscripts.

Discipline was strict at Qumran, with a hierarchy of twelve priests, three elders, a superior, and a treasurer. Excommunication was taken seriously and enforced in cases of rebellion against community discipline or lying about possessions. Yet love was the rule, and great attention was given to the daily gatherings for meals, which were regarded as an integral part of their brotherly life together. As such, Qumran presents a good parallel to many early Christian monastic communities three centuries later.

Chapter 2

The Scriptural Position, Part I:
The Old Covenant Fulfilled in the New

From the time of the patriarchs, God's plan was to have a people which would live entirely for God. God's choice fell upon the seed of Abraham, the 'children of Israel' (Exod. 3:10), the Hebrews. The way in which God led the Hebrews out of Egypt, through the wilderness, and into the Promised Land of Canaan, is pregnant with significance for the church. Egypt[1] has long been regarded as a type for this present, fallen world, and Canaan as the place of living a victorious life for God and knowing his bounties, not just in heaven but also here on earth. Israel had to come out of Egypt and become a separate people for God. On arrival in the Promised Land, it was to eradicate the nations which possessed that land, suggesting the New Testament concepts of putting off the old man (Col. 3:9-10) and putting to death what is earthly in us (Col. 3:5-6). God desires and calls a people who will come out from the fallen spirit of the age, put off the old ways, pursue holiness, and live solely for God.

Little is known of the material prosperity of Israel at the time of the Exodus, but it is likely that their poverty as virtual slaves of Pharaoh had been compensated by the spoil which they took with them (Exod. 1:14; 12:35-36). The important thing, however, was for Israel to be a people separate from the nations round about. The internal relationships of individual members of that society are only touched when involving elements which endanger their status as God's people, for example in the murmurings against Moses, the golden calf, and Korah's rebellion. That there were poor among them, however, is clear from such a verse as Exodus 23:11, a reference to the Jubilee, to which we will return. Nevertheless, the manna sent by God to feed Israel in the wilderness significantly illustrates God's egalitarian plan. All the people were able to share it, according to the need of each household. When it had been collected it was found that the one who gathered much had nothing left over, and the one who gathered little had enough (Exod. 16:18).

There are distinct echoes here for the Christian, who will remember the first church at Jerusalem, where all things were shared in common so that "there was not a needy person among them . . . and distribution was made to each *as any had need*" (Acts 4:34-35). The parallel deepens when we read of those who, contrary to God's express word, attempted to keep a secret store of manna for themselves. Moses' anger against them reminds us of Peter's wrath against Ananias and Sapphira, whose similar deceit was tantamount to "lying to the Holy Spirit" (Acts 5:1-3).

With Israel established in Canaan and able to live in peace, a pattern emerged. A nation composed of tribes and close-knit families spread over a considerable area inevitably found differences growing in levels of material and financial prosperity. Throughout the period of the old covenant it was regarded as a sign of God's honor for a man to grow prosperous and increase in flocks and lands (see Gen. 13:2; Job 42:12), while at the same time there were the poor. The Jews were not minded to change this situation by radical legislation. Indeed, they regarded it as God's order for things: "The rich and the poor meet together; the Lord is the maker of them all" (Prov. 22:2) or "The Lord makes poor and makes rich" (1 Sam. 2:7).

Although poverty was regarded in some circles as a sign of judgment and a reproach (e.g., Prov. 19:7; 14:20; Jer. 5:4), there was a basic understanding that the poor were to be accepted. They were, after all, Israelites and fellow heirs of the promises. Works of charity were to be performed and injustice stopped wherever found so that the lot of the poor might be improved. In the book of Job, for example, while it is God who meets the needs of the destitute (5:15-16), it is nevertheless an integral part of Job's blamelessness before God that he delivers and succors the poor that he finds (29:12; 31:19-20). Moreover, kings were to protect the rights of the needy (Prov. 29:14) and any who would be righteous were enjoined to consider the destitute and treat them justly (Prov. 29:7, KJV).

Jubilee

Alongside this model of private ownership, stewardship, and charity, came the highly significant concept of the *sabbatical year* and the *year of Jubilee*. The first mention of the sabbatical year is in Exodus 23:11, where God instructs the Israelites to leave their land fallow every seventh year so that their herds and the poor among them could eat of it. The parallel passage in Deuteronomy 15 elaborates on this: debts among brethren were to be annulled and a general restoration take place. According to the honesty with which this was done, God would honor with a removal of *all* poverty:

> There will be no poor among you (for the Lord will bless you in the land which the Lord your God gives you for an inheritance to possess), if only you will obey the voice of the Lord your God . . . (v. 4).

A few verses later (v. 11) comes the apparently contradictory statement that "the poor will never cease out of the land." Yet what follows is an exhortation to "open wide your hand to your brother, to the needy and to the poor." In the context of the sabbatical year this suggests a spiritual principle in shadow form: to live *at all times* the principles of the sabbath year restoration.

This notion is developed significantly in Leviticus 25 and its delineation of the year of Jubilee. After seven sabbatical years, in other words forty-nine years, the following year was to be a year of Jubilee, marked by sweeping socioeconomic changes.

The land was to lie fallow, as before, with neither sowing nor pruning, yet here there is no mention of the poor eating from the land. Rather, God will provide for all alike:

> And if you say: "What shall we eat in the seventh year, if we may not sow or gather in our crop?" I will command my blessing upon you in the sixth year, so that it will bring forth fruit for three years (vv. 20-21).

Moreover servants were to be liberated, so long as they were of Israel's stock (vv. 39-41). Debts were to be repaid and capital redistributed (v. 25 ff.). In short, a radical restoration to equality of a social and financial order which might, over forty-nine years, have grown unjust. It is surely more than coincidence that the following chapter contains the formula of the covenant in a particularly intimate rendering: "If you walk in my statutes and observe my commandments . . . I will make my abode among you, and my soul shall not abhor you; And I will walk among you, and will be your God, and you shall be my people" (26:3, 11, 12). The Lord gladly dwells among a people who will earnestly and obediently practice the highest commands of love, to redistribute all things in order to create justice and equality.[2]

A link with the ministry of Jesus is enlightening at this point, for it becomes apparent that his teachings often had a distinct flavor of the Jubilee about them. Whether or not we can confidently state that Jesus knowingly proclaimed a new and permanent Jubilee is open to debate, but the evidence is certainly tempting. At Nazareth, for example, where he made an open declaration of his anointing by God, he quotes from Isaiah 61:1-2:

> The Spirit of the Lord is upon me, because he has anointed me *to preach good news to the poor.* He has sent me *to proclaim release to the captives* and recovering of sight to the blind, *to set at liberty those who are oppressed, to proclaim the acceptable year of the Lord* (Luke 4:18-19, emphasis mine).

The parallel with the Jubilee is obvious, both in the manner of restoration outlined and in the use of the term "acceptable year of the Lord." Two verses later Jesus declares, 'Today this Scripture has been fulfilled in your hearing,' making it plain that he saw himself, as Messiah, heralding a fulfillment of the principles of the old covenant year of Jubilee.

Again, in Luke 12:22-31 we read the well-known words, "Do not be anxious about your life, what you shall eat, nor about your body, what you shall put on . . . for all the nations of the world seek these things; and your Father knows that you need them. Instead, seek his kingdom, and these things shall be yours as well." There is an evident connection, in theme and phraseology, with the Lord's answer to the anxious questioners in the Jubilee passage quoted above.[3]

Equally significant is the Lord's Prayer itself, with its central section:

> Thy kingdom come. Thy will be done,
> On earth as it is in heaven.
> Give us this day our daily bread;[4]
> And forgive us our debts,
> As we also have forgiven our debtors (Matt. 6:10-12).

Not only do we here find the same reliance on God for material needs, but we also encounter a verb often used in financial contexts. Though "forgive us our trespasses" is known by heart by millions, the correct rendering is indeed *debts*, and the verb *(aphiēmi)* has a definite sense of paying back. Indeed, the same root verb is used in the Septuagint to translate certain parts of the Jubilee passage in Leviticus 25. John Yoder points out that in Jesus' explanation in verse 14 ("For if you forgive men their trespasses, your heavenly Father also will forgive you") a different word is used, clearly signifying trespasses generally. This underlines the point that Jesus' hearers would automatically have taken the clause of the prayer in its material/financial sense.[5] Seen in this light, the Lord's own summary of prayer is firmly rooted in the Jubilee and signifies that, through him, the new age of the kingdom of God is dawning, which will operate on the lines of full restoration, justice, and equality outlined in Leviticus.[6]

Further Old Testament foretastes of the life of sharing and equality may be seen in David's egalitarian treatment of his band of followers in 1 Samuel 30, where those who waged war and those who guarded the baggage were to be equal ("they shall share alike," v. 24). The Levitical priests were to have no material inheritance in the land, because the Lord himself was their portion (Deut. 18:1-2). This suggests that in the new covenant, where all alike are priests to the Lord (1 Pet. 2:9), it should be so with all believers. The common sharing of tithes by the people under Nehemiah (13:10-13) shows marked similarities to the community at Jerusalem in Acts 4 with its deacons stewarding the common fund.

The Prophetic Movement

The last major strand in the Old Testament foretelling the life of common good and mutual sharing is that of prophecy, particularly those passages recognized as messianic. From these it is evident that the Christ will bring into being a society of justice and righteousness, where the poor and meek are upheld and transgressors punished. For example, in Isaiah 11 we read: "With righteousness he shall judge the poor, and decide with equity for the meek of the earth. . . . Righteousness shall be the girdle of his waist, and faithfulness the girdle of his loins" (vv. 4-5). Immediately follows the familiar picture of harmony and unity so often held to refer to the new earth after the last day. But in its context, it foretells a life of justice, equality, and peace brought in by the Messiah in the here and now:[7]

> The wolf shall dwell with the lamb,
> and the leopard shall lie down with the kid. . . .

The cow and the bear shall feed;
their young shall lie down together;
and the lion shall eat straw like the ox.
The suckling child shall play over the hole of the asp. . . .
They shall not hurt or destroy in all my holy mountain (vv. 6-9).

Remnant Theology and the Hasidim

In exilic and post-exilic times, the issues of poverty and justice came significantly to the fore. Israel, God's people, had been overrun, captured, exiled. What had gone wrong? A period of self-examination was to be expected, and out of it grew the protest movement of the Hasidim, who saw the nation as a whole as corrupt and rejected by God. They themselves were the faithful remnant which God had promised to leave in Israel, to atone for the sins of the nation and to receive the special mercies of the Lord.

Howard Kee cites as a prime example of this remnant theology the so-called Isaiah Apocalypse, dating to around the fourth century B.C. The nation has sinned and forsaken God's holy covenant (24:5), adopting a sensual lifestyle (a reference to the growing adoption of Greek ways by many of the wealthier Jews, known as Hellenists). God will judge this by overthrowing the whole cosmic and social order (24:1-2, 21). Yet a faithful people from within the people, the "true Israel," shall be spared on account of their righteousness (26:2) and shall know a day of resurrection and the reestablishment of the just and glorious rule of God (25:8; 26:19; 24:23). For the meantime, however, this faithful remnant is to withdraw from the common corruption, to pray and wait on God (26:20). It is significant that this faithful remnant is composed of the *poor* and the *needy* (25:4; 26:19).[8]

At first it seems that the Hasidim operated as a cell within the larger organism of Israel, foreshadowing the Christian notion of *ecclesiola in ecclesia*. But before long, groups were separating physically from the corrupt throng, to live alone in waste places as communities of true godliness and obedience. In this line stood the Essenes, with their Dead Sea community of Qumran, already discussed in the preceding chapter. The whole process is remarkably similar to the state of affairs at the close of the Roman Empire, with Christian hermits and cenobites withdrawing to the desert.[9]

In this line also came the baptizing sect of John the Baptist, an itinerant apocalyptic prophet baptizing men and women as a definite sign of repentance from the sin of Israel as a whole. Because Jesus himself describes him as the greatest man of the old covenant (Matt. 11:11), John may be regarded as somehow a culmination of the old order, an exponent of the values which God saw as the best that the old order could produce. And what were those values? "Bear fruits that befit repentance" is foremost (Luke 3:8), speaking of a radical and genuine forsaking of the old. But his words to individual groups of people reveal the Hasidic message of social righteousness (vv. 12-14), coupled with the costly giving and egalitarianism discussed earlier in this chapter: "He who has two coats, let him share with him who has none; and he who has food, let him do likewise" (v. 11). This, the pinnacle of God's righteousness among humanity, was now to find its fulfillment in Jesus the Christ.

Social Redress and the Birth of Jesus

Further links between Hasidic beliefs and the life of Jesus may be detected in the prophecies given at the time of his gestation and birth. Mary, in her psalm of praise now called the Magnificat, thanks the Lord for acting in power to bring about a social redress and a new righteousness:

> He has shown strength with his arm,
> he has scattered the proud in the imagination of their hearts,
> he has put down the mighty from their thrones,
> and has exalted those of low degree;

> he has filled the hungry with good things,
> and the rich he has sent empty away (Luke 1:51-53).

This she testifies, having already heard from the angel that the baby was to be named Jesus (meaning "God saves"), "for he will save his people from their sins" (Matt. 1:21). "His people" obviously had no sense as yet of "all people." Rather, it was to Mary simply the Jewish nation. The word *hamartia* ("sin") is the usual word for moral degeneration. Mary saw Jesus as the one who was to restore justice and righteousness to Israel.

The same reaction was in Zechariah when he exclaimed:

> Blessed be the Lord God of Israel,
> for he has visited and redeemed his people . . .
> that we, being delivered from the hand of our enemies,
> might serve him without fear,
> in holiness and righteousness before him all the days of our life
> (Luke 1:68, 73-75).

It is true that Zechariah sees more of the spiritual significance in the coming kingdom ("knowledge of salvation," "forgiveness of sins," v. 77), but he also shows that such a salvation would be lived out by the new, dynamic people of God "in holiness and righteousness"—clearly a social notion. Indeed the spiritual and the social were to be inextricably linked in the messianic message.

It has already been shown that Jesus' message had at its heart many aspects of the Jubilee. The new social order to be brought about through him, the kingdom of God, was to be a Jubilee society. People were in need of a radical and thoroughgoing change in their outlook on life. Such is apparent in the first recorded words of Jesus' public ministry: "Repent, for the kingdom of heaven is at hand" (Matt. 3:2; Mark 1:15). The word translated "repent" *(metanoeite)* has the sense of changing one's perspective, one's mentality, covering all aspects of living—spiritual, familial, mental, and material.

Jesus' Example

As if to strengthen the Jubilee idea and to lead by example in it, Jesus, the Son of God himself and heir to all the riches of heaven, adopted a life of voluntary poverty, despising personal property. As Paul puts it, "Though he was rich, yet for your sake he became poor, so that by his poverty you might become rich" (2 Cor. 8:9). His life was the perfect example of sacrifice. All that he was, all that he had, was given in service of his brothers and sisters of the house of Israel:[10] time, energy, compassion, love. As for financial and material things, he embodied the Jubilee principle. His reliance on God led to divine provision of all necessities. As he said to one potential follower (who we may assume was attached to creature comforts), "Foxes have holes, and birds of the air have nests, but the Son of man has nowhere to lay his head" (Matt. 8:20).

The same principle is evident in the call of the twelve, who were expected to leave all and follow in complete trust, and thus live in the "new mentality" of the Jubilee all the time (Mark 1:16-20; 2:14). Peter and Andrew, James and John left their fathers (family), boats (possessions), and nets (occupations). The band of disciples then traveled around with their master, sharing all with him. Sometimes they were maintained out of donations from certain followers, such as Mary Magdalene, Joanna the wife of Chuza, and Susanna (Luke 8:1-3),[11] but at all times they lived from a common purse, which was entrusted to the care of Judas Iscariot (John 12:6; 13:29).

The Economy of Jesus

What gain was there for those who so followed? Participation in the new family of God. Jesus paved the way in this regard by his own treatment of his mother and brothers:

> And they said to him, "Your mother and brothers are outside, asking for you." And he replied, "Who are my mother and my

brothers?" And looking around on those who sat about him, he said, "Here are my mother and my brothers! Whoever does the will of God is my brother, and sister, and mother" (Mark 3:32-35).

All genetic distinctions are therefore to be overcome in the messianic kingdom of righteousness. The metaphor of the family evidently bespeaks unity, equality, and common sharing. Jesus later expounds the matter in more detail to the twelve, following his pronouncements against riches:

> Peter began to say to him, "Lo, we have left everything and followed you." Jesus said, "Truly, I say to you, there is no one who has left house or brothers or sisters or mother or father or children or lands, for my sake and for the gospel, who will not receive a hundredfold now in this time, houses and brothers and sisters and mothers and children and lands, with persecutions, and in the age to come eternal life" (Mark 10:28-31).

Allegiance to the new "family" of Jesus' followers required rupture with established ties "for the sake of the gospel." In those days, family ties were a strict and rigid matter, with set roles and responsibilities, leaving no flexibility for following the Lord. (It is interesting to note that, although at first his family did not believe in him [John 7:5], Jesus' dedication to his ministry was honored by his Father to the extent that by the time of Pentecost, the whole of his surviving natural family had believed [Acts 1:14].)

The Centrality of Love

The teachings of Jesus elaborate clearly the issues involved in the common life of his followers and form the *raison d'être* for them. Foremost among them is his teaching on *love*, which he demonstrated in his acceptance of all, his eating with sinners, and his healing of outcast lepers. A key passage speaks of this love:

> And one of the scribes came up and ... asked him, "Which
> commandment is the first of all?" Jesus answered, "The first is,
> 'Hear, O Israel: The Lord our God, the Lord is one; and you
> shall love the Lord your God with all your heart, and with all
> your soul, and with all your mind, and with all your strength.'
> The second is this, 'You shall love your neighbor as yourself.'
> There is no other commandment greater than these" (Mark
> 12:28-31).

Here he cites the post-Jubilee verse from Leviticus concerning
love for one's neighbor *as oneself*. The implication is clear: just
as we do not care for ourselves simply in our thought-life but
rather in every way, by clothing, feeding, tending, and nurtur-
ing, so too must we now attend fully to the material needs of
our neighbor. The scribe in Mark 12:34, who interpreted the
Scripture just as Jesus had done and saw its essence as holy
love, was told that he was "not far from the kingdom of God."
In other words, he had the heart and disposition on which that
kingdom is founded.

The Meaning of "Neighbor"

At this point a brief excursus is necessary in order to correct a
current misconception. "Neighbor" is today almost universally
held to refer to humanity generally and Christian charity is
forever urged on that basis. This is, however, not wholly true to
Scripture. Jesus was talking to Jews, the chosen people of God.
He was *not* talking to Gentiles. In fact Jesus' conduct toward
non-Jews was, for the most part, distant. The good Samaritan
could indeed be praised, and a faith-filled centurion could find
his servant healed, but the Syrophoenician woman had to
pester Jesus relentlessly even to gain his attention. Even then
she heard her race likened to "the dogs" (Matt. 15:22-26). The
Samaritan woman at the well was likewise shown the error of
her nation's doctrine. Jesus himself said his mission was to the
house of Israel.

Now under the terms of the new covenant, the Christian

church has assumed its place as the "Israel of God," as it is expressly called in Galatians 6:16. So Jesus' ministry is to the church, not the world (John 17). This affects our interpretation of "neighbor." For example, in Ephesians Paul writes, "Let every one speak the truth with his neighbor, for we are members one of another" (4:25), which clearly limits its application to members of the church, who alone are members of the body of Christ. Likewise, in the very passage most commonly adduced for basic charity to all, Matthew 25:31-46 ("I was hungry and you gave me food," etc.), Jesus gives a summary: "Truly, I say to you, as you did it to one of the least of these my brethren, you did it to me" (v. 40). The use of "my brethren" limits the context drastically—perhaps to Jews, more probably to his disciples—for nowhere does Jesus imply that all the people in the world are his brethren. So, while honor and good works are indeed to be shown to all people (Phil. 4:5; 1 Thess. 5:15), true and full sharing in love is to be among the Christians alone, as both Peter and Paul reveal: "Honor all [persons]. Love the brotherhood" (1 Pet. 2:17). "Let us do good to all ... especially to those who are of the household of faith" (Gal. 6:10).[12]

Renunciation of All Things

Further aspects of Jesus' teaching bear directly on the life in common of his followers, not least his message of renunciation of all things. A true and committed following of him was no easy matter. It required careful counting of the cost, as is shown in the parables of the man about to build and the king contemplating battle (Luke 14:28-32). These illustrations are sandwiched between two of Jesus' least popular statements:

> If any one comes to me and does not hate his own father and mother and wife and children and brothers and sisters, yes, and even his own life, he cannot be my disciple. . . . So therefore, whoever of you does not renounce all that he has cannot be my disciple (vv. 26, 33).

Here the kingdom outstrips the Jubilee. Jesus now requires not merely a restoration to a former state of fairness, but a full renunciation of all things material and familial, indeed even of one's own will and desires. Following Christ in truth requires the enthronement of him alone as Lord of men's lives and a surrender of all idols. The episode of the rich young ruler (Matt. 19:16-22) supports this further, in that here is an apparently zealous and upright Israelite, keeping the law and desiring truth. Yet Jesus, knowing the heart, responds: "If you would be perfect [the word signifies "whole," "complete"], go, sell what you possess and give to the poor, and you will have treasure in heaven; and come, follow me." His *possessions* render him unfit for following Christ, for his loyalties will be divided. It is therefore not surprising that "when the young man heard this he went away sorrowful; for he had great possessions."

In both Matthew's and Luke's accounts this episode is followed immediately by Jesus' attack on riches (Matt. 19:23-29; Luke 18:24-30), where he declares how hard it is for a rich person to enter the kingdom of God. He sets against this the blessing of a hundredfold reward for those who renounce all things, of which mention has already been made. And as if any were still disposed to quibble, he makes the issue explicit in Luke 12:33-34:

> Sell your possessions, and give alms; provide yourselves with purses that do not grow old, with a treasure in the heavens that does not fail, where no thief approaches and no moth destroys. For where your treasure is, there will your heart be also.

The issue is starkly clear. Possessions are a snare and a source of endless anxiety. (Contrast the carefree reliance on God of the fulfilled Jubilee already mentioned.) Anyone living with possessions will find following Jesus in a truly committed fashion an immense struggle. The telling statement about our "treasure" underlines a principle later taken up by Peter, that "whatever overcomes a man, to that he is enslaved" (2 Pet. 2:19).

We can be overcome (the Greek word suggests "subordinated," "made inferior") by possessions insofar as they assume control of our thinking and motivations, thus rendering us unyielded to God. Jesus' answer is unequivocal: *sell your possessions.* Put this alongside the passage already cited, where one who does not renounce all that he has is unable to be a disciple, and we conclude that such a putting away of possessions is *not* some distant pinnacle of perfection to be attained by some, as it later came to be regarded,[13] but is a prerequisite of following Jesus at all. The renunciation of Mammon in the *heart* must be absolute and issue into a voluntary giving and sharing of possessions.

The Sin of Covetousness

In essence, the point being made here goes right back to the Fall and its root principle of *gain.* The very name of Adam's son, Cain, signifies "gain," "acquisition." The sin of covetousness is expressly outlawed in the Ten Commandments (Exod. 20:17). It was the undoing of many an Old Testament figure (e.g., Lot's wife looking back to Sodom, David's coveting of Bathsheba). It was repeatedly denounced by the prophets (e.g., Hos. 12:8; Amos 2:6-7). It was the last of the temptations with which Satan tempted Jesus and here we see clearly who is the lord of earthly possessions: "All these I will give you, if you will fall down and worship me" (Matt. 4:8-9). Jesus' reply, "You shall worship the Lord your God and him only shall you serve" (citing Deut. 6:13), is significant in that it foreshadows the message of renunciation which he was soon to bring.

The message is plain: God offers life to those who truly seek it; Satan offers the good things of this earth instead, with the motive of ensnaring and trapping people's souls irrevocably through them.[14] To gain salvation from such a situation, a full and thoroughgoing sacrifice of all possessions and worldly ties must take place. Mammon becomes an idol, even a god, which would seek to rule people's lives as surely as God would, but the choice has to be made:

> No one can serve two masters; for either he will hate the one and love the other, or he will be devoted to the one and despise the other. You cannot serve God and mammon (Matt. 6:24).

The Demonic Power of Possessions

A slight development is evident in the parable of the sower and Jesus' own explanation of it (Mark 4:3-20), where worldly possessions and the covetous heart are presented not so much as barriers to entering into discipleship, but rather as a potent force for backsliding and apostasy:

> And others are the ones sown among thorns; they are those who hear the word, but the cares of the world, and the delight in riches [lit. *seductions* of riches], and the desire for other things, enter in and choke the word, and it proves unfruitful (vv. 18-19).

Possessions easily assume demonic proportions, seducing the soul. Paul was under no illusions about this:

> Those who desire to be rich fall into temptation, into a snare, into many senseless and hurtful desires that plunge men into ruin and destruction. For the love of money is the root of all evils; it is through this craving that some have wandered away from the faith and pierced their hearts with many pangs (1 Tim. 6:9-10).

Paul's answer is that we should refuse any temptation to assimilate godliness and gain (v. 5). We should instead give ourselves fully to godliness and "contentment" (v. 6, a term with roots in "sameness" and "self-sufficiency," a communitarian word). Elsewhere Paul exhorts his addressees to "put off the old nature with its practices," having just listed as a deadly sin "covetousness, which is idolatry" (Col. 3:5, 9).

As one Christian writer so trenchantly comments, who lived in community in Czechoslovakia in the 1570s:

> Covetousness is a dangerous and evil disease, which blinds man's eyes and stops his ears; [it] lets neither the conscience nor one's own soul know salvation, for the most base matter of metal controls it and rules it.... For just as fire, when one puts much wood on it, grows greater, even so is it with covetousness: the more one brings to it, the more it raises itself up. What they have they heed not, but put it away behind them and snatch at what is before them, and before long end as Aesop's dog did.... This pestilential disease has ruined the earth; it has turned all things to confusion, so that one pines away with hunger and another destroys himself with fullness.... This crime and deceit of Belial has filled streets with blood and towns with weeping and wailing. It has drawn us away from the most blessed service of Christ, and gnaws our heart away from the Word and seed of God.... This urge made Judas a traitor, ruined Ananias and his wife, and covered Gehazi, who might have been a disciple and prophet, with leprosy.[15]

Tithes and Offerings

Jesus nowhere clearly states his position regarding the tithe, which is still the chief yardstick of giving in many Christian circles today, yet there are indications. In his diatribe of "woes" against the scribes and Pharisees, he upbraids the latter for tithing diligently, right down to herbs, yet neglecting the weightier matters of justice and mercy (Matt. 23:23). In the sequel he does not condemn the tithe outright ("these you ought to have done, without neglecting the others," v. 23b), but his point is clearly that a tithe paid by anyone not living the principles of the fulfilled Jubilee is worthless. Moreover, Jesus had already enjoined of his would-be followers that their righteousness exceed that of the scribes and Pharisees (5:20). Failure to do so precludes entry into the kingdom, a pronouncement reminiscent of his insistence on full renunciation of worldly desires and possessions already discussed.

Thus, by way of various exhortations to liberal, unstinting giving (e.g., Luke 6:35, 38), we arrive at the episode of the widow's mite (Mark 12:41-44):

> And he sat down opposite the treasury, and watched the multitude putting money into the treasury. Many rich people put in large sums. And a poor widow came, and put in two copper coins, which make a penny. And he called his disciples to him, and said to them, "Truly, I say to you, this poor widow has put in more than all those who are contributing to the treasury. For they all contributed out of their abundance; but she out of her poverty has put in everything she had, her whole living."

This incident reveals a crucial truth. Giving out of one's plenty, though not condemned, is not the fullest and truest sacrifice in the sight of God; for he demands all. Jesus' own example, living as he did with nothing to his name, was the embodiment of the new covenant Jubilee-society. Here, the widow's giving prefigures the full and spontaneous sharing of all things which was to follow the conversion of the three thousand on the day of Pentecost. The tithe remains in basis a thing of the old covenant; for in the new covenant through Jesus, *our tithe is everything we have.* How else are we to interpret the kingdom parables in Matthew 13:44-46?

> The kingdom of heaven is like treasure hidden in a field, which a man found and covered up; then in his joy he goes and sells all that he has and buys that field. Again, the kingdom of heaven is like a merchant in search of fine pearls, who, on finding one pearl of great value, went and sold all that he had and bought it.

Conclusion

The Jesus who came to bring salvation to the lost had more in view than merely to forgive sins. The words used for "salvation" in the New Testament have a rich texture of meaning: "wholeness," "completeness," "health," "deliverance." The Lord is lord of the whole of a person's being—spirit, soul, and body. He is lord of one's time, one's desires, one's possessions, and one's finances. That plan of salvation presented in the gospels begins, of course, with the removal of the legal penalty for sins and the reopening of a door to God through the blood of the Lamb.

But it goes much further. We leave the kingdom of this world, with all its ways, and are translated into the kingdom of God, with new values and responsibilities. This kingdom is the fullness of the Jubilee, a society of justice and righteousness, where all are equal, both in terms of spiritual blessing received and of material needs supplied. All alike must obey and renounce all things, following the example of the Lord who owned nothing but lived out of a common purse, relying on the promise of a faithful God to bestow on his people (corporately) all that he knows they need.

Chapter 3

The Scriptural Position, Part II: Jerusalem and Beyond

Before the Holy Spirit descended on the day of Pentecost, many indications had already been given as to how the church was to be constituted and how it was to live. Jesus' frequent exhortations that the servant was to be as his Lord and to "follow me" indicate that the church soon to be born was to continue not only the teachings but also the lifestyle of Jesus himself—as servant, as proclaimer of justice and equality, as the embodiment and the fulfillment of the Jubilee, as the first-born of a new people, the manifestation of the kingdom of God. Moreover, Jesus had declared in Matthew 16:18: "You are Peter, and on this rock I will build my church."

The Nature of the Church

The Greek term here is *ekklesia,* and only twice is it found in the Gospels, though it was to become the normal term for "church" after Pentecost. The term comes from *ek,* meaning "out" or "out of," and *klesia,* the passive form of *kaleo,* "to call." So the word suggests "those who are called out."

In the Greek world of that day (which included Israel insofar as many of its wealthier citizens—the "Hellenists"—were adopting Greek modes of life) a religious use of the word *ekklesia* was new, for it was usually a political term. At Athens, for example, it referred to the assembly of all those who had rights of citizenship. At the sound of a herald's proclamation, all these citizens would leave what they were doing and proceed to the Pnyx, the regular meetingplace for such an assembly, leaving behind all slaves, sojourners, and foreigners. Acts 19:39 uses the term in precisely this manner.

Yet *ekklesia* is also used in the Greek text of the Old Testament (the Septuagint) to render the Hebrew *qahal*, which does have a religious usage, denoting the assembly of the elect. *Qahal* refers to the gathering of the Lord's people and includes within its ambit the one who is calling—namely, God. It is clearly this association to which Jesus is alluding in Matthew 16:18 when speaking of "my church."

The church, therefore, though not yet "clothed with power from on high" (Luke 24:49), was already clearly defined in the mind of Christ. It was the gathering together of all those truly called of God. The herald had already made his proclamation in the Lord Jesus. Those who had followed the call had left what they were doing—as had Peter and Andrew, James and John—and had assembled together outside the normal run of life.[1] Such true followers are separated from the world and united in a radically new lifestyle, that of their herald and Lord.

The Two Kingdoms Doctrine

The final passage of significance in this respect is the high priestly prayer of Jesus in John 17. Here too the future nature and life of the church is sketched out. Central to it is the doctrine of the two kingdoms: that of God and that of this fallen world; light and darkness; Christ and Belial. Those chosen and called by God (v. 2) are given to Jesus "out of the world" (v. 6). They are not *of* the world, even as Jesus himself is not (v. 16). He prays for them, but not for the world (v. 9). These true believers follow his example and move in his heart, and are subjected for that reason to the same persecutions (v. 14).

Their mission is nevertheless to be in the world, not to be taken out of it (i.e., in resurrection of body). They are to present the fullness of the new life of Christ to people in order to save them also (vv. 18, 20). The constant stress is on *ekklesia*, coming apart, being separate and distinct, forming a united, alternative gathering.

Furthermore, this new society is to be fully of one heart and mind (vv. 21-23). The means to be so is already given through the Father's glory (v. 21), and as a result it is possible, indeed obligatory, for the church to be one *in precisely the same manner* (such is the sense of the Greek) as the Father and the Son (v. 22). Now the Father and the Son are not bound together by association, but are one in substance. Neither do they contribute to one another in part. Rather, the Father has given all things to the Son, who has in turn given all things to his church. Such a model of total oneness and full, sacrificial sharing was to find its pure and logical outworking at Pentecost.

The Birth of the Church

Such prefatory remarks are necessary because of the difficulties which now arise in the Acts of the Apostles. Full communal sharing is found in chapters two, four, and five, but later on, individuals seem to have owned their own houses and held possessions, contributing out of their abundance in a way reminiscent of the old covenant tithe. This apparent contradiction, coupled with ambiguities surrounding the term *koinonia* (the usual word for "community" and "sharing," but also for "contribution"), has led the bulk of Christendom to regard Jerusalem as an experiment and in no way binding on the church. Certain scholars even deny that communal sharing ever took place at all.[2] Thus, while community of goods in the early church is indeed difficult to trace *textually*, it is nevertheless apparent *spiritually* and *theologically*, in the directives of God in Old Testament and in the life and teachings of Jesus

The Day of Pentecost

The devoted followers of Jesus—about 120 in number—awaited the promised filling of the Holy Spirit. Reminiscent of Jesus' high priestly prayer, we read that they were "of one accord" (Acts 1:14), devoting themselves to prayer. On the day of

Pentecost itself (2:1) they were "all together in one place." The Lord had already worked a unity among them, which was about to be divinely energized by the Holy Spirit. After the experience of charismatic power, Peter's sermon to the crowds in Jerusalem contained the pressing exhortation: "Save yourselves from [or "out of"] this crooked generation." Three thousand persons repented and devoted themselves, among other things, to *koinonia.*

As noted previously, the root of this word is "common," but its application in Scripture is broad. It denotes a share in the common interests and experiences of Christians. For example, it includes participation in suffering (Phil. 3:10), in knowledge of God and the Son (1 John 1:3-7), and in the ministry of proclaiming the gospel (Phil. 1:5). It is also applied to the common sharing of the bread and wine (1 Cor. 10:16). Negatively it is used for Christians wantonly abusing the covenant meal and "having fellowship with" demons.[3] Furthermore, *koinonia* is an action. It is the term given to the "contribution" made for the Judean Christians by the churches of Greece and Asia.

Precisely which application is in view in Acts 2:42 is not certain, but it is probably intended as a blanket designation for the sharing of all things, experiential, spiritual, and material.

The material sharing is immediately explained in the ensuing verses and in a parallel passage in chapter 4.

> So those who received his [the apostle Peter's] word were baptized, and there were added that day about three thousand souls. And they devoted themselves to the apostles ' teaching and fellowship, to the breaking of bread and the prayers. And fear came upon every soul; and many wonders and signs were done through the apostles. And all who believed were together and had all things in common; and they sold their possessions and goods and distributed them to all, as any had need. And day by day, attending the temple together and breaking bread in their homes, they partook of food with glad and generous hearts, praising God and having favor with all the people. And the Lord added to their number day by day those who were be-

ing saved (Acts 2:41-47).

Now the company of those who believed were of one heart and soul, and no one said that any of the things which he possessed was his own, but they had everything in common. And with great power the apostles gave their testimony to the resurrection of the Lord Jesus, and great grace was upon them all. There was not a needy person among them, for as many as were possessors of lands or houses sold them, and brought the proceeds of what was sold and laid it at the apostles' feet; and distribution was made to each as any had need (Acts 4:32-35).

A New Haburah

The community thus inaugurated by the Holy Spirit was organized along the lines of a *haburah* (a voluntary association common among the Jews), central to which was a communal meal. As F. F. Bruce points out, the phrase "in their homes" (v. 46) is better rendered "by households," a reading borne out by early papyri. The three thousand Jews would have come from far and wide for the Pentecostal festival and would not have had homes in Jerusalem. So those already resident as citizens took in numbers of the remainder and lived as *haburot*, celebrating the Lord's Supper and sharing goods and possessions.

The Western text of Acts, a manuscript variant, renders verse 45 thus: "And as many as had possessions and goods sold them and parted them daily to all, according as anyone had need," suggesting that capital was turned into hard cash and *contributed* on a daily basis to those in need. Some have seen this confirmed in 4:32: "No one said that any of the things which he possessed was his own, but they had everything in common." This suggests individual retention by title of possessions, while in point of fact they were shared or donated.

Surrender of Capital

This, however, runs contrary to 4:34-35 where the impression is given of a full, sacrificial surrender of capital and funds at the apostles' feet, thus creating a common pool out of which the needs of all could be met. This would seem the more likely explanation, given the appointment of the seven deacons in Acts 6, whose task it would be to ensure equality and justice in the daily distribution (v. 1). Are we really to suppose they went round to all the five thousand (4:4) in turn, daily, to ask how much they had donated and to work out whether that was fair? Evidently they were appointed to steward the common fund of the donated goods and possessions of all the believers.

The quibbling has continued for centuries over the correct interpretation, one group favoring full sharing, another stewardship. Certainly there was not one great, definitive sale of everything. As Jackson and Lake point out in their study of Acts, the verbs used are in the imperfect tense, suggesting that *they followed a policy of selling possessions.* As each new member joined, he or she would sell, deposit, and share. Such, after all, was the example of Jesus, the outcome of his ministry, the heart of his prayer, the truest reflection and outworking of a heart of love now united with brothers and sisters in a new society.[4]

For this reason Peter was able to say to the cripple in the Beautiful Gate of the Temple, "Silver and gold have I none." Here, "silver and gold" stands for financial means generally. They had voluntarily put away the hold of mammon by sharing all things with others. Barnabas had done the same, selling a field and donating the entire proceeds (4:36-37).

Ananias and Sapphira

But now we come to the episode of Ananias and Sapphira, which has proved a frequent stumbling block to our understanding of the Jerusalem community:

> But a man named Ananias with his wife Sapphira sold a piece of property, and with his wife's knowledge he kept back some of the proceeds, and brought only a part and laid it at the

apostles' feet. But Peter said, "Ananias, why has Satan filled your heart to lie to the Holy Spirit and to keep back part of the proceeds of the land? While it remained unsold, did it not remain your own? And after it was sold, was it not at your disposal? How is it that you have contrived this deed in your heart? You have not lied to men, but to God." When Ananias heard these words, he fell down and died (Acts 5:1-5).

What are we to make of the suggestion in this passage that it was not obligatory to sell property? Did only the most spiritual Christians do so? Ananias may have wished to be regarded as one of those. Yet it is more likely that this verse simply underlines the voluntary nature of the sharing at Jerusalem. Nobody was coerced into parting with goods or selling property, for the very suggestion would be contrary to the Spirit of Christ, who emptied himself (Phil. 2:7) unconditionally, holding nothing back from his beloved, being one with them as his Father was with him. The tithe had been relegated from a commandment to a desirable standard for the devout in Jesus' day, and now in the church it seems that Jesus' command to "sell your possessions" (Luke 12:33) was interpreted not as something into which to bludgeon the unwilling, but as a natural outflow from—indeed as a proof of—a heart renewed in love by the Holy Spirit.

Thus, even after Ananias had made the sale, he was still free to donate or not, as he pleased. How that is to be interpreted is uncertain, for it cannot mean that he would automatically have ceased to be a Christian had he refused to donate anything. Yet crucial to our understanding of it all is Peter's use of the term "keep back" (v. 3). The Greek *nosphizo* has the sense of "embezzle" and is found in the Septuagint denoting the sin of Achan (Josh. 7), who kept some of the devoted things of Jericho which the Lord had forbidden Israel to touch.

The parallel is the more striking because of the point at which the episodes occur in Israel's and the church's history. For Israel it was the initial advance into the Promised Land, the reaping of long-awaited promises, calling for obedience and full reliance on God. Achan transgressed through covetousness and Israel met with defeat at Ai. Only after the sin had been rooted out and Achan and his family stoned, could God's honor again be with his people. Similarly the church of Acts moved in the first flush of Spirit-given energy to reap the promises of the Lord. Ananias and Sapphira transgressed, again through basic covetousness, and God's judgment was equally fierce. After all, what they were seeking to retain was mammon, the pit and snare discussed above. As such, their action revealed hearts that were already, in essence, backsliding from true love.

Conclusion

The picture thus gained from the first chapters of Acts is one of the firstfruits of true *agape* love, where the Holy Spirit fulfilled at once the old covenant jubilee overtly. Jesus had previously fulfilled it in his own person. In his high priestly prayer, he prayed that his brothers and sisters might be fully one. The "one heart and soul" of 4:32 is one indication that this purpose of God was being fulfilled. The new life in the heart which Jesus brought to individuals in regeneration was finding a natural and logical expression in the love of all who had become partakers in that salvation. The society of justice and equality of the Jubilee was fulfilled at Jerusalem. Again, the facts are not always easy to extract textually, but spiritually, even theologically, the Pentecostal community of goods was fully the mind of God and an integral part of his redemptive plan.

The Beginning of Persecution

The first community enjoyed the favor of all the people (2:47a). After all, the Romans would have regarded them as a sect within Judaism, which was a *religio licita*, a tolerated faith. To the Jews, these "followers of the Way," as the Christians seem to have been known from the outset (19:23, with evident reference to John 14:6), were a *haburah* of the sort familiar in the city. Moreover the fruits were good: people were healed, their lives were changed and God was being glorified.

Yet the tide turned when it was seen that central to this new faith was the Jesus of Nazareth only recently executed as a criminal, whom these "Christians" (the name first appears at Antioch, several years after Pentecost, 11:26) were proclaiming as the Messiah. Though they continued to attend the prayers and festivals of the Temple, they spent all the time they could in their exclusive household gatherings. Suspicion, jealousy (the numbers of converts were startling), fear, and outraged ancestral piety led to opposition.

Stephen, the first martyr, was stoned to death. "A great persecution arose against the church in Jerusalem; and they were all scattered throughout the region of Judea and Samaria, except the apostles" (8:1). Central to the persecution was Saul of Tarsus. Just how severe it was is clear from Saul's own subsequent testimonies: "I persecuted this Way to the death, binding and delivering to prison both men and women. . . . When they were put to death I cast my vote against them. And I punished them often in all the synagogues and tried to make them blaspheme; and in raging fury against them, I persecuted them even to foreign cities (22:4; 26:10-11). Luke himself speaks of Saul as 'breathing threats and murder' (9:1). In such an environment of unrest and fear for one's very life, no home was free from the danger of a sudden raid. Thus, the prospects for full communal living and sharing were not exactly good. Among the Christians in this first dispersion, the common life of sharing was therefore continued on a more flexible basis. This is clear from the episode of Philip and Simon Magus which directly follows the account of Saul's persecution and which must therefore have taken place during that period. Simon believed, became a Christian, and was baptized (8:13), though as yet he had not received the Holy Spirit. From the offer of money made to Peter (from which the term "simony" derives), we learn that he had funds at his own disposal. Evidently the uncertainty of the times precluded any full-scale common purse.

This all took place in the early A.D. 30s. What happened when the persecutions subsided and Christians could breathe again is largely a matter for conjecture. Luke's account dwells on two notable conversions, namely the Ethiopian eunuch, a servant of royalty, and Cornelius, the God-fearing Roman centurion. Luke also emphasizes signs and wonders and the spread even further of converts as a result of Saul's persecutions.

New Hardships

Whether many made attempts to rejoin the twelve at Jerusalem is uncertain, but they would have had little comfort, for in A.D. 44 a double blow hit the city. Herod Agrippa, puppet king of the Jews, sought to give Jewish morale a boost by fomenting further persecutions against the Christians. James the son of Zebedee, one of the twelve, was martyred. Peter was arrested but miraculously freed by an angel. With the increased hostility, the believers could only huddle together and pray. One place where they gathered was "the house of Mary, the mother of John, whose other name was Mark." Some have seen in this phrase evidence that by now even large possessions such as houses were in private hands. Yet it is as hard to prove this as it is to prove the contrary, that citizens of the city took in others to share their home and to have all things in common with them. We just do not know.

The second blow was the famine foretold by the prophet Agabus (11:27f.). Historically this is well attested. Suetonius records that the reign of Claudius was marked by regular droughts and crop failure. Of this particular drought, dated to A.D. 46 under the procuratorship of Tiberius Julius Alexander,

Josephus records that Judea suffered so badly that Helena, queen-mother of a pagan king, send her servants abroad to buy grain and figs for famine relief in Jerusalem. Surprisingly, despite the evidence, some have maintained that the Jerusalem church fell into severe financial straits because of its community of goods. Yet it is clearly evident that the now much-depleted community was having to spend its meager resources on the sheer necessities of living.

It is in this context that the believers outside Judea decided to make a donation for the relief of Jerusalem's need, each contributing "according to his ability" (11:29). It seems that the contingency measure of believers retaining a certain amount of capital amid the uncertainties of persecution, was now coming to be regarded as the norm. Yet we must not be misled by the Greek, translated here "according to his ability," which literally has the sense of "as any thrived." There is no indication here of a basic inequality with some prospering and others not. Rather it speaks of *earnings*, which will always differ from one to another. The actual donation of it, wherever a need presented itself, would have been unquestioned.[5]

The Jewish problem dogged Claudius throughout his reign. Historical accounts and several preserved letters reveal him gradually losing patience with the Jews on account of their frequent riots and unrest. That Christianity had already reached the capital by this stage is beyond reasonable doubt, for when Priscilla and Aquila arrived at Corinth from Rome, they were already believers. To the Romans, mainstream Judaism and Christianity were still indistinguishable. So the Jewish hostility to "the Way" must, to them, have seemed like a pointless feud. Twice Claudius was forced to legislate against the Jews in Rome. In 41 he forbade them to meet together. In 49 he banished them from the capital altogether, as is borne out in Acts 18:2.

Hence there can have been little sympathy in the empire for Jewish Christians at this point, who found themselves tarred with the same brush as their orthodox kinsfolk. Again we infer that it would have been extremely difficult, if not imprudent, for Jewish Christians to live and share communally at this time. Priscilla and Aquila had their own dwelling at Corinth (18:3) and Paul was able to stay with them (as Apollos did later), but there is no evidence of a residential community on the Jerusalem model.

And what of the Gentile converts, who did not have to contend with such hostilities? We may reconstruct from the third missionary journey (e.g., 21:4, 7) that in any place Paul's band reached, they could seek out "the disciples" and stay with them. This, at the very least, suggests that the Christians lived in close proximity in one area of the town, presumably in or around the house where they held their meetings. Yet in verse 8 we read that Philip and his family had their own house at Caesarea, where they gave hospitality to Paul. It is inconceivable that inequality between Jewish and Gentile Christians would have been tolerated, so we assume that Gentile converts too kept their houses and practiced hospitality and sharing out of their abundance. Not quite the high standards of the Jerusalem community in its bloom.

Evidence from Paul's Epistles

The bulk of our evidence for the later interpretation of "all things in common" comes from the epistles. To our knowledge, Paul had not known Jesus, nor had he inside experience of the community of goods as practiced in the first church. By the time he met Christians in his converted state, it was in Gentile Damascus where the believers were living in fear of their lives. Therefore Paul experienced the sharing life of community as sacrifical giving and mutual support from individually retained purses. It was an "emergency measure," not the norm. However, he seems to have adopted it without difficulty and without attempting to restore a common purse as at Jerusalem.

Yet his vision was for equality, justice, and partnership. Ephesians 4:28, for example, exhorts converted thieves to work with their hands so that they may have something to share with one in need. Certainly the way in which Paul was interpreting "all things in common" was less clear-cut than that at Jerusalem, and more open to abuse by human selfishness. But his stress is on *liberality* and *sacrifice* as the root of all giving.

This is especially apparent in the passages concerning the contribution for the saints in Judea. 1 Corinthians 16:2 implies that each believer did indeed retain his money, but now each was to put aside a certain amount every Sunday and save it until Paul arrived. In his following letter, Paul is able to comment on this giving and on the heart out of which it came. The giving was joyful and costly, for the churches of Macedonia were poor themselves (2 Cor. 8:2). Their giving amounted to a "wealth of liberality," for they had given *beyond* their means, actively begging to be able to contribute for the needs of their sisters and brothers (vv. 3-4).

There is no doubt that Paul saw in this a sign of God's fruit and blessing, for elsewhere he is keen to lead by example in gratitude and joy when in receipt of a financial contribution. The Philippians had sent aid to him at Rome, having previously done the same when he was at Thessalonica. Paul responded, "I am filled, having received from Epaphroditus the gifts you sent, a fragrant offering, a sacrifice acceptable and pleasing to God. And my God will supply every need of yours according to his riches in glory in Christ Jesus" (Phil. 4:18-19).

Stewardship, liberal giving, sacrifice, and gratitude are therefore the characteristic features of Paul's stance. Yet was he *advocating* individualism with regard to possessions or merely tolerating a system already in being and which by now could not easily be changed? Certain facts suggest the latter.

In Philippians 4:15 he bemoans the fact that no church other than Philippi had been willing to "enter into partnership of giving and receiving" with him (the verb is *koinoneo*, with its suggestions of "in common"). Paul does not specify what he means here, but the context is strictly financial. He is also keen to admonish the rich among the believers to "be communioners"—to distribute (the root is *koinoneo*) for the good of their souls (1 Tim. 6:18). And he enjoins on everyone hospitality and the practice of sharing of all things (cf. Rom. 12:13, where the literal sense is "distribute to the needs of the saints"—*koinos*—by sharing all things in common).

Paul frequently refers to the "church in the house." In Romans 16 Priscilla and Aquila, now at Rome, have such a gathering, as do Asyncritus, Phlegon, and a group of believers. Philologus, Julia, and a few more do as well (vv. 5, 14-15). There has been much debate on how to interpret this, whether as a meeting place for services or as a residential arrangement. From 1 Corinthians 14:23 we see that the whole church met together only irregularly, suggesting that at other times, as in Acts 2, the believers met "by households." In microcosm the daily life of love, meeting, and sharing together took place in the households. Wherever a Christian owned a property, others entered with him or her in that "partnership of giving and receiving." All things were held in common, though facts are lacking to prove that there was a common purse.[6]

The General Epistles

Other New Testament writers agree, but with less detail. James inveighs against the rich in a manner reminiscent of the Lord (esp. 5:1-6), stressing the principles of justice, righteousness, and brotherly love. To claim faith but not to share with one's brothers and sisters, he points out, is of no profit (2:15-16). Indeed, John says it is a sign of unregeneration (1 John 2:11; 3:10). Peter points out that the false prophets who will lead many astray will be characterized by greed and covetousness (2 Pet. 2:1-3, 14b). It is hard to interpret his exhortation to "love one another earnestly from the heart" (1 Pet. 1:22)—or indeed Paul's great passage on *agape* love in 1 Corinthians 13—outside of a communitarian setting. John echoes the parable of the sower in his solemn warning against the world, whose destructive evils he sums up as the lust of the flesh, the lust of the eyes, and *pride in goods* (literal translation, 1 John 2:16). And while the writer to the Hebrews can speak of the believers as having property (10:34), his clear word a little later is, "Do not neglect to do good and to share what you have" (13:16).

Conclusion

The impression nevertheless gained is of a gradual acceptance of lower standards in the interests of flexibility in an uncertain social and political environment. The way presented and lived out by Jesus, in fulfillment of Jubilee and prophecy, was one of total, absolute sharing—of interests and labors, time and experience, and of material necessities through a common purse. His statement that "you always have the poor with you" (Matt. 26:11) is pre-Pentecostal, addressed to persons who had not as yet received the Holy Spirit.[7] To such he enjoins charitable giving of alms out of one's plenty.

But once the Holy Spirit had descended and had inscribed the law on the hearts of the disciples, as Jesus had said he would, the immediate and natural fruit was a common purse, a full and sacrificial sharing of everything in fulfillment of the Jubilee principle. And while James, in his letter, can stress the fact that charitable giving to widows and orphans is still the heart of true religion (1:27), a higher and truer way had now been introduced by the Spirit: a giving of *everything*, as the widow had her mite and as Jesus had demonstrated in the example of his own life.

Chapter 4

From the Close of the New Testament to Constantine

From the patristic writings (texts by early church fathers after the close of the New Testament period), developments can be traced in the interpretation and practice of the common life. It is important to note from the outset, however, that passages dealing specifically with poverty, sharing, and brotherly love are comparatively few. Apparently, such matters, particularly in the early years, were taken largely for granted and needed no specific statement. Instead, under attack from heresy, the pens of the fathers were occupied with matters of basic doctrine.

Nevertheless, it is clear that one major theme of early Christian outreach was that of a *new society* through Jesus, which lived a new lifestyle along lines that ran counter to those of the world around it. The early second century *Preaching of Peter* and the late second century *Ad Diognetum* both refer to the Christians as "a third race" or a "new race." It was this very distinctiveness that was anathema to the sacralism of Rome and paved the way for the first charge against the Christians— *odium generis humani*—literally, "hatred of the human race." To Rome, any who refused allegiance to the religion of the empire could only be spies and conspirators.

The way in which this common life of sharing was lived out seems to have varied according to time, place, and social condition. A full pooling of goods and income as at Jerusalem was not always evident. Rather, the pattern of stewardship and liberal giving was more the norm. Unquestioned throughout was the belief that love should lead in all things and spur to generosity in all giving. For example, Clement of Rome, the first bishop of that city, wrote around A.D. 90, "Let the rich man supply the wants of the poor, and let the poor man give thanks to God because he has given him someone to supply his need."[1] The inherent separation of Christians from the values of society around, however, meant that such liberality of giving did, in fact, happen. It was regarded as a vital part of the testimony of the gospel, helping to maintain a society of visible justice and righteousness. Tatian, in his *Address to the Greeks,* writes about how Christians make no distinctions in rank and outward appearance, wealth and education, or age and sex.[2]

The Second Century

The call to share all things in common was still heeded, however, as various writings prove. Justin Martyr's *First Apology,* dating from before 150, states, "We who formerly treasured money and possessions more than anything else now hand over everything we have to a common treasury and share it with anyone who needs it."[3] The second century *Epistle of Barnabas* reiterates the apostolic pattern exactly in its exhortation to the "new people" that God had called: "Use all in common with your neighbor and do not say it is your own; for if you are partners in what is eternal, how much more are you partners in what is temporal?"[4]

Tertullian, in his *Apology* of c. 198, states:

> We form one body because of our religious convictions, and because of the divine origin of our way of life and the bond of our common hope. . . . So, we who are united in mind and soul have no hesitation about sharing what we have. Everything is in common among us, except our wives. In this matter, which is the only matter in which the rest of mankind practices community, we dissolve our sharing![5]

He goes on to explain that the believers lived off the bare minimum needful for food and clothing and, on a given day of the week, gave the surplus to the common treasury for the aid of the aged and infirm, or for persecuted brothers and sisters.

Perhaps the clearest exposition of "all things in common" is to be found in the *Instructor* (or *Christ the Educator*) of Clement of Alexandria, dating to around 190. In the twelfth chapter he writes:

> It is God himself who has brought our race to possession in common first of all by sharing himself, by sending his Word to all men alike, and by making all things for all. Therefore, everything is common, and the rich should not grasp the greater share. The expression, then, "I own something, and have more than enough. Why should I not enjoy it?" is not worthy of a man and does not indicate any community feeling. The other expression does, however: "I have something, why should I not share it with those who have need of it?" Such a one is perfect, and fulfills the command: "Thou shalt love thy neighbor as thyself" (Matt. 19:19). . . . I admit God has given us power to use our possessions, but only to the extent that it is necessary. He wishes them to be in common. . . . How much more honorable it is to serve many than to live in wealth! . . . How much more useful to have friends as our adornment than lifeless decorations! Who can derive more benefit from lands than from practicing kindness?[6]

This makes an interesting comparison with an extract from a Jewish text of a generation earlier, the *Mishnah:*

> There are four ways of thinking among men. The average man says, "What is yours is yours and what is mine is mine." The naive man says, "What is mine is yours and what is yours is mine" [in the sense of a straight exchange]. The false man says, "What is yours is mine and what is mine is mine also." The godly man says, "What is mine is yours and what is yours is yours as well."[7]

The Third Century

In the third century the pattern is still evident. Stewardship was the norm, but constant admonitions were given to liberality and communal sharing. Certain pseudo-Clementine writings (probably of this date but falsely attributed to the Clement already quoted) show that there was an ever-present groundswell of feeling in favor of full sharing. For example, in the *Homilies* (xv: 9), St. Peter supposedly says to Clement:

> If we, who have chosen the future things, possess many goods, be they clothing, food or drink, or any other thing, we possess sins, because we ought not to own anything. To all of us, possessions are sins.[8]

A work whose date has long been uncertain but is probably of the early third century, the *Didache* (or *Teaching of the Twelve Apostles*), has this to say:

> You shall not turn away the needy but have all things in common with your brother; you shall not say it is your own. For if you are partakers in the eternal, how much more are you partakers in the perishable?[9]

The *Didache* also contains a passage on the communion bread, likening its union of grains that were once "scattered over the hills" to the union of hearts that should be among Christians gathered together in sharing love. The passage inspired an Anabaptist pen many centuries later, which produced this development of it:

> As the grain kernels are altogether merged, and each must give its contents and strength into the one flour and bread, likewise also the wine, where the grapes are crushed under the press and each grape gives away all its juice and all its strength into one wine. Whichever kernel and whichever grape, however, is not crushed and retains its strength for itself alone, such a one is unworthy and is cast out. This is what Christ wanted to bring home to his companions at the Last Supper, as an example of how they should be together in such a fellowship.[10]

It is hard to envisage such a complete oneness of heart and life outside the full sharing of true *koinonia*.

At this period there arose a group taking the name of Apostolici, who lived in the regions of Phrygia, Silicia, and Pamphylia. They held to the way of separation from the world in a rigorous manner, rejecting private property as an evil snare to the soul—a practice which sometimes gave them the name Renunciatores. Little more is known of them, however, except that St. Basil still knew some of them in the late fourth century at a time when he, too, was living in community.[11] The Apostolici were preceded in the Phrygian area by the Montanists, a sort of charismatic movement which sought to reestablish the moral rigor and spiritual gifts of former days. Though prophetic, their lifestyle was marked by a return to strict asceticism and liberal giving. Tertullian, whose communitarian sympathies have already been noted, felt no hesitation in joining them around A.D. 207.

The Tragedy of Constantine

Early in the fourth century a development took place which was to change the course of church history entirely. Central to it was the figure of Constantine I. Son of the emperor, he was brought up at the court of Diocletian at just the time when the Byzantine idea of absolute rule was gaining favor over the older idea of joint emperors. Proclaimed emperor at York, Constantine nevertheless had to fight for his rights and secured the imperial purple only after a bloody battle at the Milvian Bridge in 312. What was so significant was that Constantine attributed his victory to the God of the Christians. He had seen a vision on the night before the battle of the Greek letters *chi* and *rho* intertwined. These were explained to be the initial letters of "Christus." Furthermore, Constantine heard a voice saying, "In this sign, conquer." He therefore made his soldiers carry the motif on their shields, and duly won the victory.

The result was that the Christians, who only a few years earlier had suffered their worst persecution under Diocletian, now came to be regarded with favor. In fact, when Constantine and his co-emperor Licinius met at Milan in 313, they made Christianity, a *religio licita*—an officially sanctioned faith. The persecution stopped and Constantine's evident favor for their beliefs meant that the Christians gained something of an upper hand. There was, however, a terrible price to pay. Constantine spent the remaining years of his life attempting to tie the church to the state as closely as possible. The pagan Byzantine notion of the emperor as absolute ruler, combined with the Roman idea of his being "pontifex maximus" (high priest) convinced Constantine of his right to be head both of the state and the church.

The desirable political by-product of a united empire would also not have escaped his shrewd mind. Effectively, however, he was reintroducing the very "one society, one faith" principle which Jesus and the apostles had sought to overturn. Any citizen of the Roman Empire had a right to be counted as a member of the Christian church. And although the decree whereby Christianity became the sole religion of the empire did not come until the rule of Theodosius I in the 380s, the upshot was that the distinction so clearly drawn by Jesus between the kingdom of God and the kingdom of this world became hopelessly blurred.

It was not as though Constantine's innovation was backed up by a life worthy of the Lord he now claimed to know. While legislating often in favor of Christians, he also allowed pagans to build shrines. He forbade soothsayers and mediums to enter private houses, but allowed them to pray if the imperial palace was ever struck by lightning. The altar of Victory was not removed from the Senate house and for several years pagan motifs continued on coinage. Worst of all, the very man who in 325 convened and presided over the famous Council of Nicea, the very next year ordered the murder of his own wife and eldest son for callous political reasons—this from a man who was hailed as "bishop of bishops" and "the equal of the apostles"! Nor did he consent to be baptized until seriously ill and near death.

The effect of the state-church merger was an inevitable drop in standards of biblical righteousness. One recent scholar[12] has made the useful distinction between the true, gathered, regenerate "body of Christ" and the new, diversified, all-embracing "body of Christendom." While some saw the latter as an unexpected bonus from the Lord and spoke of it as a "deeper fulfillment" of the purposes of God (the phrase is Augustine's), the true body of Christ found its task severely hampered by the massive influx of worldly, nominal people. The problem was that the emperor severely repressed any divisions and schisms. Thus the church could not afford to offend the compromisers.

The Death of Normative Communalism

In such a bewildering climate, the church had to assimilate the call to the common life of sharing to the vast organism of the new, cosmopolitan state church. To suspend any form of common sharing was unthinkable, since it was central to the Master's teaching on practical love, yet to impose the sharing of possessions on the whole empire by imperial decree was impracticable. Furthermore, the newfound stability in the empire seemed to hail the return of former prosperity,[13] and people were becoming more materialistic.

So something of a debate ensued. Never formal, it was more a collection of random voices. Arnobius (early fourth century) took the conservative line, speaking of Christians as those who "prefer the friendship of Christ to all the things of the world."[14] Lactantius, on the other hand, while a worthy champion in many areas, saw the sharing of all things in common as positively undesirable. He feared such sharing would breed irresponsibility and laziness and, as in Plato's ideal society already cited, tend toward vice and the sharing of wives.

A Double Standard

Yet, to prevent disunity in Christendom, an answer had to be found. Therefore, so as not to undermine the state church's foundation, a compromise solution was reached whereby the renunciation of all things and sharing possessions in common were idealized for a few. Thus, the sharing originally enjoined upon all was put on a pedestal and presented as the highest way, though too high for most. This was not exactly new, if we accept a statement attributed to a bishop named Archelaus at the end of the third century. Replying to a question from a certain Manes about how to interpret Christ's call to renounce all things, Archelaus said, "I reply that it is a good thing *for those that are capable of it*, but at the same time to employ riches for the work of righteousness and mercy."[15] In other words, it was permissible to hold wealth and use it for God, but gone was any sense of the biblical challenge: "Whoever of you does not renounce all that he has cannot be my disciple" (Luke 14:33).

Thus a convenient double standard was invented of gross proportions. But it was just what the Constantinian order needed. It was taken up and publicized widely. Cassian, in the late fourth century, propounded a two-tier system of Christian living, with giving up all as the higher way. His contemporary, Augustine, who himself lived in community, admits much the same in his 355th sermon:

> Notice how we live. In our community, no one is permitted to own anything, though possibly some do. It is permitted to no one, so if some do own property, they do so without permission. However, I think well of my brethren, and since I maintain this good opinion, I have omitted any enquiry into the matter.[16]

Yet perhaps the clearest indication of how the commands of Jesus were now being interpreted in a way that blunted their cutting edge, is to be found in the writings of John Chrysostom.

He knew and valued the early church pattern of "all things in common" and discussed it at length in his *Homilies on the Acts of the Apostles:*

> They did not give in part, and in part reserve; . . . they removed all inequality from among them, and made goodly order. . . . If this were done now, we should live more pleasant lives, both rich and poor, nor would it be more pleasant to the poor than to be the rich themselves. . . . Should we not make it a heaven upon earth?

He goes on to bid his hearers accompany him on an imaginary journey to the Pentecostal community as it shared all goods and possessions, savoring its holy love and power. But, aware of the acute discomfort such a journey could involve, he interposes an assurance: "I said, only in imagination, so let none get excited, either rich or poor!"[17] He had accepted the double standard, and says so explicitly in his *Homilies on St. John* of around 390:

> What, therefore, did Christ say? "The foxes have dens, and the birds of the air have nests, but the Son of Man has nowhere to lay his head." If, then, we should require this of you, it would perhaps seem to most of you burdensome and inconsiderate. Therefore, *because of your weakness* [my emphasis], I dispense with this exact imitation, but I do not expect you to be attached to wealth. . . . I do not censure those who have houses, and fields, and wealth, and slaves, but I wish you to possess these things . . . as you ought. . . . You did not receive wealth for this reason, that you might bury it, but that you might distribute it. If God wished it to be stored up, he would not have given it to men, but would have permitted it to remain lying in the ground. However, since he wishes it to be expended, he therefore permitted us to have it, that we might share it with one another.[18]

He concludes with the neat compromise that it is permissible to have possessions so long as we do not let them possess us.

Minority Objections

Yet there was a reaction. Individual churches throughout the empire continued to view the stewardship-or-sharing debate and choose their stances. Some in Syria seem to have preserved the radical tradition of having all in common for the sake of one's fellow believers. They saw that a creeping compromise was pervading the church as a whole. Materialism and nominalism were combining to erode spirituality, especially in financial matters. The tendency was therefore growing to pay lip-service to common sharing, but not to practice it. As a reaction, an unknown Syrian father wrote these lines of prophetic indignation, which are preserved in the so-called *Apostolical Constitutions:*

> He that has money and does not bestow it upon others, is like the serpent, which they say sleeps over treasures; and of him is that Scripture true which says, "He has gathered riches of which he will not taste"[19] and they will be of no use to him when he perishes. For such a one has not believed in God, but in his own gold. Such a one is a dissembler, a respecter of persons, unfaithful, cheating, fearful, unmanly, shallow, worthless, a complainer, ever tormented, his own enemy, and nobody's friend.[20]

The only true and honest answer, continues the writer, is to share what one has with those in need, with the orphans and the widows, who in turn ought to receive such support "with all fear and in pious reverence."

Chapter 5
The Early Middle Ages

At the time of Constantine's decree in the second decade of the fourth century, there were already many believers who were disenchanted with the worldliness of the church at large and who longed for a life of true devotion to God. Sensing that matters would go from bad to worse in a huge, all-embracing "body of Christendom," they saw the only answer as lying in a retreat from the world altogether. Over an area from Egypt to Palestine numerous hermits withdrew to the desert to dwell in caves, pray to God, and live by faith.

The Desert Fathers

Others held to the Lord's word that he would *gather* his people, and sought to draw the hermits together into little communities. One such person was an Egyptian named Pachomius. He had tried the life of the recluse but found it unfulfilling. So around 320 he gathered together several hermits in the Thebaïd region of Egypt and founded a community where all things were shared. His aim was to provide, through God's grace, a way of life where the spiritual and physical hazards of the solitary hermit's life were overcome. Only in mutual commitment did he see this as possible. All was to center on love for the brothers and sisters and devotion to Christ.

His move proved so fruitful that it spread rapidly. Hundreds of disenchanted Christians, longing for a common life of separation, withdrew to the desert communities. In his lifetime Pachomius founded nine communities for men and two for women. The communities were segregated on the grounds that celibacy was the higher way and that mingling the sexes was too much of a temptation.

These "desert fathers," as they became known, drew up a rule to govern their lifestyle. It stressed three essentials: obedience, labor, and communal sharing. Prayers and meals were held together, while the daily round centered on devotions, tilling, planting, copying books, and receiving visitors. By 350 the communities housed thousands[1] and were centers of power. Many stories of healings, miracles, and exorcisms were attributed to Pachomius and others, such as Theodore and Anthony.

The fragmentary writings of these desert fathers reflect the profound sense of blessing they felt in their communal living, which they always referred to as *koinonia:*

> It is by the favor of God that the holy *koinonia* appeared on earth . . . by which he made the apostolic life known to men desirous of modelling themselves after the apostles.[2]

> We are the children of the holy vocation of *koinonia.* . . . We thank God, the Father of our Lord Jesus Christ, for having made us able to forget our pains and distresses by the sweet fragrance of the submission and solidity in faith of the rule of holy and true *koinonia.* . . . We have surrounded ourselves with the wall of salvation, which is love for the law of God and for the vocation to *koinonia,* that we might walk upon the earth according to the ways of the company of heaven and the life of the blessed angels; so that all who see our good works will glorify God and know that we are disciples of Christ, since we truly love one another without hypocrisy.[3]

St. Anthony observed the rise of the new Constantinian system with its mistrust of separation, and foresaw an inevitable drop in standards of godliness: "A time is coming when men will go mad, and when they see someone who is not mad, they will attack him, saying: 'You are mad, you are not like us!' "[4]

These *cenobites,* as those living in community came to be known, stood as a testimony to the honor of God on those returning to their first love and to the social righteousness of the first church. While the original hermits had stressed the *individual* virtues of holiness and self-denial, the cenobite communities stressed the more *social* virtues of humility, patience, and mutual love.

Beyond the desert in the Christianized empire, the predominant stance on possessions remained that of stewardship. The writings of Ambrose of Milan (339-397) are fairly typical. He did not question a person's right to private ownership, but he did strongly attack riches. He also introduced the concept of *restitution:*

> It was in common and for all men, rich and poor, that the earth was created.... Nature knows no rich, she produces only poor: we are born without apparel and come into the world without gold and silver.... It is not what is your own that you give to the needy, but what is his that you are restoring; for it is a common good, given for the use of all, that you alone are usurping.[5]

Augustine and the Rise of Monasticism

The call to a full sharing of all things was not, however, totally absent. Several bishops began to open their homes to others, usually elders or deacons, to live together in community. The first known to do this was Eusebius of Vercelli, who died in 370. Their example spread widely. The most notable figure involved was Augustine, who began community living as soon as he arrived at Hippo in North Africa, his home for the next forty years. In his *Sermons* (nos. 355, 356) he speaks much of the foundation of this living which began in 395:

> All, or nearly all of you, are aware that we live in the house that is called the Bishop's House and that we follow the example, as much as we can, of those holy men who are mentioned in the Acts of the Apostles: "Not one of them said that anything he possessed was his own, but they had all things in common...."

> I was looking for a place to establish a monastery and live in
> community with my brethren.... I brought nothing.... I
> started to gather brethren who were well disposed as my
> colleagues, men who possessed nothing, as I had nothing, and
> who followed my example. Thus, as I sold my meager estate
> and gave it to the poor, so also did those who wished to live
> with me; our purpose was to live in community.[6]

Augustine also drew up a rule for the nunnery presided over
by his sister. It enforced full sharing of possessions and distribution to any as needed (Epistle 221). Elsewhere he goes as far as
to say that withdrawal from community sharing was to
renounce one's claim to faith in Christ.

Koinonia as the Energizing Impetus for Monasticism

His example was followed by many from North Africa to the
Black Sea, as a reaction set in to the material complacency of
the new Constantinian state church, even among those who
had no intention of leaving it. And as the move to the
monasteries progressed, many arose to commit to paper the
heart that lay behind such a step. At the turn of the fifth
century John Chrysostom wrote, in his *Homilies on the Acts of
the Apostles:*

> If we retain them [our possessions], we shall fail to achieve great
> things, and instead become a laughingstock to the spectators
> and to the evil one himself. For even if there were no devil, and
> nobody to wrestle with, yet ten thousand roads on all sides
> would lead the lover of money to hell.... Here the devil has
> no hand in the work, we do it all ourselves.[7]

And again in his *Homily on 1 Timothy* he writes:

> Is not this an evil, that you alone should have the Lord's
> property, that you alone should enjoy what is common? Is not
> "the earth the Lord's, and the fullness thereof"? If then our
> possessions belong to one common Lord, they belong also to

our fellow servants. The possessions of one Lord are all common.... [God] hath made certain things common, as the sun, air, earth, and water, the heaven, the sea, the light, the stars, whose benefits are dispensed equally to all as brethren. We are all formed with the same eyes, the same body, the same soul, the same structure in all respects, all things from the earth, all men from one man, and all in the same habitation.... Other things he hath made common, as baths, cities, marketplaces, walks. And observe, that concerning things that are common there is no contention, but all is peaceable. But when one attempts to possess himself of any thing, to make it his own, then contention is introduced, as if nature herself were indignant, that when God brings us together in every way, we are eager to divide and separate ourselves by appropriating things, and by using those cold words "mine" and "thine." So those greater things he hath opened freely to all, that we might thence be instructed to have these inferior things in common.[8]

His contemporary, John Cassian, agrees entirely:

If one is walking along the course previously marked out [friendship in the common life], how can he ever differ from his friend, for if he claims nothing for himself, he entirely cuts off the first cause of quarrel (which generally springs from trivial things and most unimportant matters), as he observes to the best of his power what we read in the Acts of the Apostles on the unity of believers: "But the multitude of believers was of one heart and soul, neither did any of them say that any of the things which he possessed was his own, but they had all things in common."[9]

It is not always remembered that two of the most illustrious of the fathers lived in community and championed the common life of sharing. Augustine of Hippo, to whom the church owes so much on a doctrinal level, lived in a shared house, as noted previously. In his book, *The Work of Monks* (A.D. 402), he defines the heart of the early monasteries:

[A monk] has devoted himself to the charity of the common life, intending to live in companionship with those who have one heart and one soul in God, so that no one calls anything his own but all things are held in common. . . . What should be the disposition of a citizen of that eternal city, the heavenly Jerusalem, except that he should hold in common with his brother whatever he gains with his own labor, and that he should receive whatever he needs from the common supply, saying with him whose precept and example he has followed: "As having nothing yet possessing all things."[10]

St. Basil

His contemporary from Cappadocia, Basil the Great, justly revered in the Orthodox churches, also lived in community and wrote about the life in common at some length. In a letter he gives an autobiographical account of his pilgrimage to community:

> Having mourned deeply my piteous life, I prayed that guidance be given me. . . . Having read the gospel and having seen clearly there that the greatest means for perfection is the selling of one's possessions, the sharing with needy brethren, the complete renouncing of solicitude for this life, and the refusing of the soul to be led astray by any affection for things of earth, I prayed to find some one of the brethren who had chosen this way of life, so as to pass with him over life's brief and troubled waters.[11]

He had been led toward such a stance by the example of his sister Macrina, who had grown so disenchanted with the way of the world that she had withdrawn to the family's estate at Annesi in Pontus. Here she lived with her mother and all the household servants, in full equality with possessions shared. So touched was Basil that he set up a community house for men on the opposite bank of the river. Basil spent the rest of his days in community and wrote extensively about the life in common. In his *Ascetical Discourse* he writes:

The most important thing, and the chief concern for the Christian, ought to be the stripping from himself of the varied and diverse movements and passions toward evil by which the heart is defiled. The renunciation of possessions is of obligation to him who aspires to this sublime way of life, inasmuch as anxiety and solicitude for material interests engender much distraction for the soul. Whenever, therefore, a group of persons aiming at the same goal of salvation adopt the life in common, this principle above all others must prevail among them: that there be in all one heart, one will, one desire, and that the entire community be, as the apostle enjoins, one body consisting of various members (1 Cor. 12:12). Now this cannot be realized in any other way than by the enforcement of the rule that nothing is to be appropriated to anyone's exclusive use—neither cloak, nor vessel, nor anything else which is of use to the common life, so that each of these articles may be assigned to a need and not to an owner.[12]

In the *Long Rules* Basil writes, in a section entitled "On the Necessity of Living in the Company of Those Who Are Striving for the Same Goal":

If we who are united in the one hope of our calling (Eph. 4:4) are one body with Christ as our head, we are also members one of another (1 Cor. 12:12). If we were not joined together by union in the Holy Spirit in the harmony of one body, but each of us chose to live alone, we would not serve the common good in ministry according to God's good pleasure, but would be satisfying our own passion for self-gratification. How could we, divided and separated, preserve the mutual service of members or our submission to our head which is Christ?. . . In addition, since no one has the capacity to receive all spiritual gifts, but the grace of the Spirit is given proportionately to each, when one is living alongside others, the grace bestowed on each individual becomes the common possession of his fellows. . . . When several persons live together, each enjoys his own gift and enhances it by giving it to others to share, besides reaping benefit from the gifts of others as if they were his own. *Community life offers more blessings than can fully and easily be told.*[13] (emphasis added)

Gregory of Nyssa

Another fourth century text of importance for early monasticism is the treatise *On the Christian Mode of Life*, attributed to Basil's brother, Gregory of Nyssa. Its particular interest lies in the light it sheds on the difficulties and uncertainties experienced by those seeking to enter community living. All alike looked at Acts 2 and 4. But was this the blueprint for all time? Had social conditions changed to the point where the model needed modification? Thus, *On the Christian Mode of Life* takes the form of the reply of a wise and experienced Christian leader to a group of novices who ask several questions.

His answers reveal that the prime motivation behind communal living and sharing is obedience to God and love for one another, that it can only spring up when each individual heart has first come to a meeting with God and an experience of regeneration, and that its goal is the achieving of that purity of heart that shall see God (Matt. 5:8). The community's way of life is to be based on imitation of Christ—obedience with joy, humility and simplicity, the mortification of vanity, and providing for the needs of the brothers. Each member must "disdain the things that are revered in this life" and "adjust himself spiritually to his brothers in God." Gregory of Nyssa saw a progression of virtue taking place through the life in common:

> Simplicity gives way to obedience, obedience to faith, faith to hope, hope to justice, justice to service, and service to humility.[14]

As for the leaders, their duty was to be an example in all these virtues:

> It is necessary for those in charge in matters of supervision to work harder than the rest, to think humbler thoughts than those under them, and to furnish their own life as an example of servitude to the brothers, looking upon those entrusted to them as a deposit of God.[15]

Such love, humility, and service, then, was the heart of early monastic community life.

Finally, around 500, a treatise entitled *Contemplative Life* was penned by Julian Pomerius, abbot of an association of clerics living in community at Arles in France. In it he speaks of the monk as "gaining possession of spiritual goods in place of the carnal goods he has renounced." Furthermore,

> it is expedient to hold the goods of the church and to despise one's own possessions through love of perfection. For the wealth of the church is not one's own, but common; and, therefore, whoever has given away or sold all that he owns and has become a despiser of his own property, becomes a steward of all the church possesses. [16]

This is significant in that it presents a pattern of Christian stewardship altogether more challenging than that of personal stewardship so popular since. The Christian is meant to be freed from self-interest by renouncing his or her own goods in order to take part in the *corporate stewardship* of the common pool of goods in community.

This pattern continued in many lands for many decades. Sozomenus, in his history of the church (c. 425), tells of the diocese of Rhinocorurus in Egypt, where among the pastors "there is a common house and a common table, moreover they hold all things in common." [17] Paulinus, bishop of Nola, near Naples, lived in community with a number of monks and carried on an extensive correspondence with other communities. In one of his letters he warned against greed, adding: "Money is not lasting and must be enjoyed in common, for there is no eternal possession of private property." [18] In France bishops Baudin, Rigobert, and Gregory of Tours founded communities in their homes. And in sixth-century Spain, several of the councils of Toledo endorsed community living in the bishop's house. The band of missionaries active in Ireland with St. Patrick (c. 390-460) shared everything in common, as did those of Columba on

Iona and Columbanus, who travelled from Ireland to the Continent.

The instructions given to Augustine of Canterbury by Pope Gregory in 601, as he prepared to bring the gospel to England, make interesting reading. It had been customary in the Roman Church at large for the church's income to be divided four ways: to the poor, for the lodging of guests, for maintenance of clergy, and for repair of buildings. Now, however, Gregory instructed Augustine:

> You must establish the way of life practiced by our fathers in the communities of the early church, where none called anything that he possessed his own, but they had everything in common.[19]

Benedict of Nursia

Gradually the monastic and cenobite movements became more standardized, organized according to the particular rule (constitution) that they followed. Jerome translated that of Pachomius into Latin for those who wished to follow it. Others drew up their own.

Most influential by far was that of Benedict of Nursia, who had lived as a hermit before founding a community along Pachomius' lines, whose rule he expanded. This was at Monte Cassino in around 525. Benedict was uncompromising concerning the sharing of possessions, advocating a regular search of beds, lest any personal effects be hidden away. Chapter 33 of the rule asks whether a monk may have anything of his own and answers categorically: "This vice ought to be utterly rooted out . . . for monks should not have even their bodies at their own disposal." Chapter 34 asks whether all should receive necessaries in equal measure. The answer refers back to Acts 4:35—"as any had need"—adding:

By this we do not mean that there should be respect of persons—God forbid!—but consideration for infirmities. He that needs less, let him thank God and not be discontented. He that needs more, let him be humbled for his infirmity and not made proud by the mercy shown to him. So will all the members be at peace.[20]

If anyone was found to treat common property in a slovenly way, he was to be exhorted. If one was discovered to be keeping secret possessions, he was to be reprimanded and, in case of failure to amend, put under church discipline.

The Demise of the Common Life

Other programs of organization were carried out, including a major one by bishop Chrodegang of Metz in the eighth century. Yet these proved, in the long term, to bring difficulties. The early, joyful foundations of Augustine or Basil came to be hidebound institutions where the Holy Spirit found no channel to move. Some communities lapsed from sharing altogether.

Some, however, saw this as disastrous and sought to correct it, as is clear from writings preserved in what are known as the *Pseudo-Isidorean Decretals* of about 850. One was supposed to be the fifth epistle of Clement of Rome, the first bishop of that city, ordained by Peter himself. It is outspoken in its urge to share all things in common. "Clement" knows the apostles personally, it claims, and it is their wish and institution that property should be held in common everywhere. One extract reads:

A common life is necessary for all, especially for such as fight blameless for God and desire to follow the life of the apostles and their disciples. For truly in this world things should be held in common by all men. But through acquired wickedness, one saith: "That is mine," and another, "That is mine," and thus hath a division taken place among men—but not out of the counsel of God. Therefore hath the wisest of the Greeks said and recognized: "Just as the sunlight cannot be divided, and the air—even so should one have all other things in common in this life, and not divide them."[21]

He then quotes Psalm 133 and the example of Acts 2 and 4.

Another of the forgeries is the supposed *Epistle of Urban I*, who was pope c. 222-230. Here the intention is to present as authentic a warning against an abuse which the writer saw creeping into the church in the ninth century:

> We know that you are not ignorant of the fact that hitherto the principle of living with all things in common has been in vigorous operation among good Christians, and is still so by the grace of God; and most of all among those who have been chosen to the lot of the Lord, that is to say, the clergy.... Out of these common possessions, the bishops, and the faithful as their stewards, ought to furnish to all who wish to enter the life in common all necessaries, as best they can, so that none may be found wanting among them.... The property of the church, not being personal but common and offered to the Lord, is to be dispensed with the deepest fear, in the spirit of faithfulness.... Therefore, if any one now or in future times shall rise up and attempt to divert that property, let him be smitten with the judgment [of Ananias and Sapphira] already mentioned.[22]

Though now proven to be forgeries and largely disregarded, these *Pseudo-Isidorean Decretals* are nevertheless important in that they reveal that somebody, or more probably a whole group of believers, felt this message to be the word of God for the church of the ninth century.

The Rise of Nonconforming Separatists

While all this was going on, there were movements in Christendom which saw a different answer to Constantine's amalgamated state church. Rather than stay in it and live monastically, they sought to separate from it and set up churches composed solely of the regenerate. They ordained their own ministers and separated from the spirit of the age, which they saw as corrupt and in the bond of the devil. Groups such as the Paulicians of Asia Minor, the Donatists of North Africa, and the Bogomils of Hungary, from the fourth to the ninth century, held to the belief that the true church should be "without spot or wrinkle" *now*. And this they put into practice in a common life. Few sources exist concerning these groups, other than diatribes from their opponents, so it is hard to reconstruct whether they shared goods and possessions in common. But there is evidence that mutual aid and liberal contribution (at the very least) were characteristic of them. It is sad to note that Augustine became one of their most ardent foes. In terms of wholehearted devotion to God, separation from worldliness, and true love for one another, they were in full agreement. Only the great stumbling block of allegiance to the state church caused division and eventually persecution.

Chapter 6

The Late Middle Ages

Over the decades, monastic life continued to flourish, although always open to the danger of over-organization. In some orders, ecclesiastical red tape clogged the vitality of life. Throughout the bulk of the Catholic Church, there was no impetus, let alone obligation, to the life in common. So the eleventh century saw something of a reaction.

Eleventh Century Progress

A movement arose among some of the eminent bishops which pressed Rome to state its position regarding community living. Pope Nicholas II set the wheels in motion, coining the term "regular clergy" (or "regular canons") to denote orders where "all things in common" was practiced, and "secular clergy" where it was not. Twenty years later Gregory VII made moves to enforce communal sharing on all monastic orders, stressing that "the common life, as the Roman Church understands it, is where the goods of the church are employed for the common good."[1] The result was an upsurge in communal zeal in the monastic orders, especially in Germany and Austria, where bishops Altman of Passau and Gerloh of Reichersberg actively championed it. Such fervor continued for a century in many places.

However, in various lands the reform produced no lasting effects. The saintly bishop Ivo of Chartres, who died in 1203, lamented:

> Community living has completely disappeared from the churches ... and the cause must be attributed not to authority but decadence, because the love has grown cold that seeks to have all things in common.[2]

A good example of this renewed fervor in the common life is furnished by the Cistercians, who in the twelfth century founded the great houses of Cîteaux, Clairvaux, Rievaulx, and others. St. Bernard, the foremost figure of the movement, used to liken the common life to teeth: all masticate together for the good of the body. So, too, should monks.

More insight, however, is to be gained from his contemporary, Aelred of Rievaulx. Aelred likened the move into community to the Exodus from Egypt and described its life and heart thus:

> Each of you, my brothers, before coming here, had a soul that belonged to him alone. You have been converted to God, and behold, the Holy Spirit . . . has reached your souls and out of all your hearts has made one heart and soul. This soul, our community, has all the virtues of the angels, and above all, that unity and concord thanks to which . . . what belongs to each individually belongs to all and what belongs to all belongs to each. . . . No one says or presumes that anything is his own, but all things are common to all. This is to be understood, brothers, not only for our cowls and robes, but much more of our virtues and spiritual gifts. . . . Whatever (gift) each one has he should consider as belonging to all his brothers. . . . Indeed, Almighty God could immediately bring to perfection anyone he pleases, and give to each one all virtues. But his loving provision for us is such that each one needs the other, and what anyone does not find in himself, he has in the other.[3]

Aelred and his brethren saw life in common as being more God's will than the solitary life of the hermit. He took the analogy of the three-days' journey that Pharaoh allowed Israel to make, and likened it to three stages. Many achieve the first, which is separation from the world. Some attain the second, which is renunciation of evil practices. Yet because they depart and live alone, and do not share all they have with their brethren, they have not completed the third stage.

One delightful passage from Aelred exemplifies the bond of

joy and love found in community. One day, walking past his
brethren as they were sitting in the cloister, he records:

> I found not one in all that multitude whom I did not love and
> by whom I was not confident that I was loved. I was filled with
> a joy so great that it surpassed all the delights of this world. For
> I felt as though my spirit was transfused into all of them and
> that the affection of all had passed over into me, so that I said
> with the prophet: "Behold how good and pleasant it is when
> brothers dwell together in unity."[4]

The notion still prevailed, however, which we met with John
Chrysostom, namely, that only a select few are capable of at-
taining the heights of sharing all things in common. The Middle Ages crystallized this into a sharp distinction between the
religious (those in monastic orders) and the *laity* (those who
had taken no vow). Life in common was seen only as the pre-
rogative of the regular religious. The lay folk could look to
them for guidance and could join them if so led, but the idea of
a lay community was not a current one.

The Beguinages

Yet there were lay movements which felt called, nevertheless, to a common life along semi-monastic lines. One such
movement began in the thirteenth century at Oignies-sur-
Sambre. Several women were seeking an alternative to the two
usual ways of living for Christ in the Catholic Church. One
either joined a religious order or lived the life of a hermit or an-
chorite. These women began to live together and share their
goods and possessions under the spiritual guidance of a con-
fessor, Jacques de Vitry. Their avowed aim was the recovery of
the simplicity, love, and poverty of the early church. This they
practiced by giving to the poor, sharing what remained,
worshiping and praying together, and carrying on various jobs:
washing, needlework, silk spinning, bleaching, and carding.

The movement grew quickly and spread to parts of Germany and Holland, and to Switzerland, where the sisters were known as Sisters of the Forest, though its center remained Belgium. These sisters became known as Beguines and their communities as Beguinages, after Lambert le Begue (died 1187), their supposed founder. As they grew more organized they adopted the monastic pattern of a superior for each community house. By 1400 there were houses in most towns, with 6 to 50 members. They instituted schools for the local poor (resulting in a high average literacy among the Beguinages), helped widows and single mothers, and ran an infirmary.

An equivalent institution for men was started, though it never achieved the success of the Beguinages. The Beghards, as the men were known, were usually poor craftsmen who lived communally while pursuing their trades: pottery, masonry, carpentry, weaving, and smithery.

Technically each could retain his or her possessions, but in reality they were shared. The Beghard constitutions list "attachment to possessions" as one of the grounds for expulsion of a member. The Beghards were ridiculed as "poor boys" or "poor valets" and ran into hostilities with the craftsmen's guilds, whose monopolies they threatened. Finally they were ordered to be rounded up and killed by the Council of Vienna in 1311 on the suspicion of false doctrine. Thousands died at the stake while dispersed Beghards traveled as far as the Alps and Poland. Although very small in number, Beguinages still exist in Belgium (in 1933 there were 11 left and less than 1,000 members). Their legacy to Belgium is undeniable and their covenanted, sharing institutions are remembered with affection and pride.

The Waldensians

As the Beguines spread abroad, they came into contact with groups of believers from an earlier movement of great vigor, the Waldenses (or Vaudois). Their founder, Peter Waldo, or Vaudès (c. 1140-1218), was a rich merchant of Lyon in France. One day Waldo heard the story of an early Christian father who gave up everything and lived a life of absolute poverty, serving the poor. Inspired by this, Waldo used some of his money to pay for a translation of the Scriptures into the vernacular and gave the rest away, throwing handfuls of coins into the street, much as Francis of Assisi was to do a generation later. As he did so, he declared: "I am avenging myself upon these enemies of my life who have enslaved me, so that I cared more for gold pieces than for God and served the creature more than the Creator."

Waldo began to tour as an itinerant preacher. Many, especially the poor, joined him to form a society which had as its goal the poverty and sharing of apostolic days. His aim was to present the life of full surrender, separation, and voluntary poverty as open to all, not merely to the "religious." They took vows and called themselves "brothers," but far from being enclosed, the Waldenses were vigorously evangelistic. Their apostles traveled in pairs with a staff and a minimum of clothing, preaching the kingdom of God. They were ridiculed as "poor boys," "humble ones," or "sandal-wearers."

Such was the appearance of the two envoys who came to Rome in 1179 to solicit an audience with the pope during the third Lateran Council. They were seeking official sanction for their order. An English monk named Walter Map examined them, concluded that they were "idiotic and illiterate," and summed up the salient points of their faith: itinerant preaching, poverty, and community of goods, through which they sought "in poverty to follow the Christ of poverty."[5]

Attempts to find favor with Rome continued to fail, since Rome sensed an unwillingness to submit fully to the pope. Finally in 1184 the Waldenses were condemned as heretics for that very reason and their case was handed to the Inquisition. Several inquisitors left reports of their findings. Waldensian believers were tortured and their villages devastated throughout the thirteenth century. They were constantly accused (despite the communistic sharing of the regular monastic orders) of holding "all things in common."[6] For the most part, however, the accusations concern practice rather than doctrine. Waldensian writings certainly bear out their orthodoxy.[7]

In toto, they present the picture of a zealous lay reform movement, well versed in Scripture and concerned with the worldliness of the prevailing ecclesiastical system. Amid intense persecution, the Waldenses grew and expanded until their congregations spread from Bavaria to Flanders. One inquisitor even cried in despair that "one third of Christendom was Waldensian."

Certain differences in approach to possessions were encountered during this expansion, so a two-tier structure was developed: the "society" and the "friends."[8] The former required a lengthy period of probation, after which all worldly property was to be formally renounced and life in common embraced. The latter category allowed possessions to be retained so long as there was liberal giving. All alike were strongly trained in the Scriptures and spent much time learning whole sections by heart. Often an illiterate artisan could recite much of Luke's Gospel and expound the Apostles' Creed. One inquisitor admitted that he dreaded nothing more than a dispute with a Waldensian.

Gradually the number of those holding all things in common decreased, but for those remaining in that category it was strictly imposed. All preachers, teachers, and similar ministers were to live by this rule, which they saw as obligatory for any ordained minister of any denomination in order to maintain oneself morally blameless before men. Enemies regularly suspected evil in the practice, but one Waldensian named Giovanni explained that the reason why goods were shared in common was not to "buy souls" (such had been the inquisitor's allegation), but to assist the poor, be they Waldensian or not, in the love of Christ. Even the inquisitors reluctantly had to admit that they were devout, upright, and honest in their manner of life:

> They are recognizable by their customs and speech, for they are modest and disciplined. They take no pride in their garments, which are neither costly nor vile. . . . They live by their labor as artisans. Their teachers are cobblers. They are chaste, temperate, and restrain themselves from anger, avoiding baseness and light speech, lies, and oaths.[9]

Waldensians still exist today, though without any communitarian basis other than of an ethnic kind. They are even active today in the ecumenical movement, the idea of which would have horrified their twelfth-century ancestors.

The Waldensian legacy was great. The Reformed denominations all acknowledged their worth in the sixteenth century. But perhaps the greatest tribute is indirect: the growth, a generation or so after Waldo, of the Catholic orders of the Franciscans and Dominicans, who were (particularly the latter) to present Rome's answer to Waldensian methods. They, too, were to travel in pairs in simple garments. They, too, were to castigate worldliness. They, too, were to embrace poverty and hold all things in common.

Other Fringe Groups

One or two fringe groups about which little is known also seem to have practiced "all things in common" in the twelfth and early thirteenth centuries. The measures of Frederick II against heretics in 1239 are the only source for a sect in Lombardy called the Communists. All that is known is that they shared their possessions. Some eighty years before, there was a sect at Cologne (referred to in a letter to Bernard of Clairvaux of 1146) which condemned infant baptism, purgatory, transubstantiation, prayers for the dead, and private property.

This sect criticized the church at large for being so given to worldly dealings that it had lost its vitality and blessing. At the same time, around Périgueux in France, a man named Pons headed a group which held to apostolic poverty, the renunciation of riches, and evangelical outreach. Nothing more precise is known about this group than that it included monks, nuns, and even noblemen.

Throughout this period there were ample social reasons for a reaction against property and riches. In many European lands the feudal state was still alive and well, with callous rich and wretched poor. As with Negro slaves and their "spirituals" some centuries hence, many voiced to God their plea for a system of justice and love. In fourteenth-century England, for example, where barons were taking over common land and walling it into their estates, an anonymous writer penned *The Prayer and Complaint of the Ploughman unto Christ* (based on the well-known *Piers Plowman*):

> Whoever lives by love, possesses thy goods in common for the good of his neighbor, and not for himself. O Lord, since all the good that men have comes from thee, how dare any give thee of the worst and keep to himself the best?[10]

A Carmelite friar named Henry Parker wrote in his *Dives and Pauper* of 1493:

> [At the time of the apostles] all things were common to the multitude of all Christian people . . . and therefore saith the law: that common life is needful to all men, and namely to them that would follow the life of Christ's disciples.[11]

Brethren of the Common Life

Moves toward active community living increased at this time. In the Low Countries in 1374 one Gerhard Groote opened his house to several poor believers. From this grew the Christian community known as the Brethren of the Common Life, which spread over much of Holland, Belgium, and North Germany. Though organized along monastic lines, it was a lay movement, composed of men and women living in community, sharing all possessions and resources. All members practiced manual labor—dairy farming, crafts, needlework, and book-copying. The community also took in poor orphans from the society at large to educate them.

Daily life centered around manual work, fellowship, and meetings for worship. Each member was encouraged to burst forth in prayer or praise, even at work, if he felt so inspired. Dress was simple, as were the meals. After supper in the evening, time was spent in relaxed brotherhood together before retiring for the night. The confessed aim of the community's living was to practice brotherly love and "to purge our poisoned hearts from sin." The way was uncompromising. Visitors were welcome, however, and special meetings held for enquirers, who were exhorted to "extinguish vice, acquire virtue, despise worldly things, and fear the Lord." Among members there was also active mutual correction.

Each community was self-sufficient, governed by an elder (or "superior"). Each had its own librarian, physician, nurse, tailor, and bookkeeper. The elders met often. Once a year they all came together, some traveling many miles to do so. Anyone seeking to join the community was given time to "count the cost." If his desire was for commitment, he had to renounce all claim to personal possessions before a lawyer. Once a member, he was to give himself to growth in humility and brotherly love.

The spirituality of the Brethren of the Common Life is well known through their most famous writing, *The Imitation of Christ*. It may also be seen in these lines from one of its members:

> All were to approach as near as possible to the life of the apostles and of the primitive church of Christ, so that in the

whole congregation there should be one heart, and that no one should consider or call anything his own. . . . They were to love their neighbor with due charity and assist the poor. To their spiritual fathers in all lawful concerns they should yield unquestioning obedience, considering that their highest merit consisted in charity and submission. All earnings from their labor in common or in private they should, according to the apostolic rule, lay at the feet of the superior. [12]

At the same period (late fourteenth century) an anonymous mystical treatise was composed near Frankfurt by a priest of the Teutonic order. Called the *Theologia Germanica* (or *Theologia Deutsch*), it achieved immense popularity. This work presented poverty of spirit and surrender to God as the essential prerequisites of sanctification in Christ. One of the aids to this yieldedness is the overcoming of self in the area of goods and possessions:

Were there no self-will, there would be also no ownership. In heaven there is no ownership. Hence there are found content, true peace, and all blessedness. If any one there took upon himself to call anything his own, he would straightway be thrust out into hell, and there would become a devil. Where one will have self-will, there is all manner of misery and wretchedness. So it is also here on earth. Thus, he who hath something, or seeketh or longeth to have something of his own, is himself a slave . . . to what he desireth or hath; and he who hath nothing of his own . . . is free and at large and in bondage to none. [13]

Rome came under increased sniping from all manner of evangelical figures, especially Wycliffe and Huss. Churches were seceding from Rome in order to be separate from the world, and communal sharing often sprang up naturally.

One example comes from fifteenth-century Bohemia. In 1409 a politician named John Jesenic was advocating a form of government that would be truly just and where governors would prefer divine laws to human. The only model, he felt, was the early church: "Thus it would be necessary for the republic to return to evangelical polity, with all things held in common. Then we would be content with having food and clothing, and would be following the Lord's counsel."[14] The followers of John Hus agreed and took in 1415 a practical step toward its realization.

The Taborites

Several believers founded a settlement at Tabor on the Lužnice River and pledged to share all things in common. Hundreds were involved while thousands of adherents, who did not actually join in the sharing, flocked from far and wide to attend services and celebrations. At one such service in July 1419, there were an estimated 42,000 souls present. One hostile witness had to admit, "They wished to live in imitation of the primitive church, and they had all things in common. Each called the other brother, and one provided what another lacked. Meeting in peace, piety, and brotherly unity, they shared even eggs and crusts of bread with each other."[15]

The teachings of Tabor are clear from the report of a disputation in 1420. One section states: "All shall be equal as brothers and sisters.... As in the town of Tabor there is no 'mine' or 'thine,' but all is held in common, so shall everything be common to all, and no man own anything for himself alone."[16] The settlement itself consisted of huts of wood and clay arranged in clusters with little sense of planning. The men were largely weavers and wool carders, while the women performed domestic duties. Further settlements followed, at Wonian and Pišek, where one horrified opponent recounted in 1429: "The Taborites contrived a monstrous trick, enjoining all the people to bring, each one, all that he possessed and thus almost completely filled two storehouses which they had set up."[17] These communal stores were administered by chosen stewards. The sharing was total, for Tabor stressed its belief that personal ownership was a grievous sin.

The Hussite wars finally doomed the community. Repeated crusades were sent by Catholic lands to subdue the Bohemian Hussites, and the Taborites joined in taking arms to defend their heritage. At a decisive battle in 1434 they were overrun and thousands were slain. The few who escaped no longer dared to live in sharing community, for fear of further reprisals. Thus a visiting Catholic in 1451 could write with misplaced triumph:

> This people wished at one time to live in all things in conformity with the primitive church, and held all their possessions in common. Each called the other brother, and what one lacked he received. Now, however, each lives for himself alone and they suffer hunger. Short-lived was the fire of brotherly love![18]

Chelčický and the United Brethren

Yet remnants of the former communities gradually reformed, and within twenty years another community had sprung up in Bohemia. Appalled at the interdenominational violence, a former monk named Rehor (i.e., Gregory) toured the land in search of Christians of true heart who wished to lead a quiet and separated life for Christ. Helped by an impoverished knight named Peter Chelčický, he acquired some land at Kunwald, near Seftenberg, in 1457, and laid the foundations of a communitarian settlement, trusting that its pacifist nature would guarantee a better fate than Tabor.

Men and women of all social backgrounds united to build up the community. They wrote to a bishop named Rokycana: "As we knew not where to turn, we turned to God in prayer and besought him to reveal to us his gracious will in all things. We wanted to walk in his ways. We wanted instruction in his wisdom. And in his mercy he answered our prayers."[19]

The form the answer took was life in common. Chelčický did not, in fact, condemn property in itself, but apostolic poverty was his ideal: "If man were not deceived by avarice, why should he need property or take any heed of earthly things?"[20] At Kunwald the solution was full sharing, with communal houses, workshops, and farms. Agriculture was the chief occupation along with some trade. The settlement was pastored by a Hussite minister, Michael Bradacius, and assisted by twenty-eight elders.

A synod held near Rychnov in 1464 outlined three classes of membership of the United Brethren, as the wider movement came to be called. The "Perfect" were pastors, teachers, and lay persons who had renounced all things; the "Learners" were the ordinary members; and the "Beginners" or "Penitents" were probationary members. Only those in the first group were under vow to hold all possessions in common. Others could operate a stewardship system, but full renunciation was always presented as the highest way:

> Priests and those who teach should give an example to others in word and deed. . . . Also in material concerns some have come to a common decision to renounce such things, to hold nothing of their own, neither private property nor money nor any other thing, according to the example of the first Christian leaders, about whom it is written that they held all things in common, having nothing of their own but sharing all with those in need. For it is right and proper that those who are called to Christ's service should be abstemious [sparing] in their eating and modest in their dress.[21]

Those retaining possessions were exhorted: "Let them do with them as the Gospels ordain, giving to the poor. And, having shared all their goods, let them earn their bread with the labor of their hands." The "poor" was understood predominantly as those of their own congregation. Detailed instructions were drawn up regarding the manner in which such goods were to be shared: each member could either choose to whom he would distribute, or leave the distribution in the control of a trusted steward.

Gradually a decline set in. Laypersons increasingly kept possessions, leaving the ordained ministers alone to live in apostolic poverty. The only exceptions were converts of noble extraction for whom it was felt prudent to renounce all things without exception as a public sign of social justice. The issue continued to be debated into the 1490s and beyond, while persecution raged around the Brethren, forcing them often to hide in caves. Finally the Reformation brought peace and some were drawn into the larger communitarian enterprise of the Hutterites of Moravia, to whom we shall return.

Chapter 7
The Reformation

The sixteenth century was, of course, a time of intense religious ferment. Protest against abuses in the Roman Church finally erupted in an open revolt that was to change the face of Christendom. The reformers—Luther, Zwingli, and later Calvin—broke away from hidebound tradition and sought to return to the basis of Scripture. The doctrine of justification by faith swept away many unscriptural practices of Catholicism, and the "priesthood of all believers" concept finally broke the stranglehold of the clergy on the church's government and life.

But once the initial euphoria of newfound freedom had calmed, Luther and his allies had to work out the forms their new wineskins were to take. Although Luther's early vision was for a disciplined, voluntary church, he finally adopted the Constantinian model of old, seeking to embrace everyone in the new Protestant Church just as Rome had hitherto embraced all within Catholicism.

There were many believers, however, who considered this a great mistake. The Reformers, they claimed, had not gone far enough. One writer pictured Luther as a man trying to mend an old kettle but succeeding only in making the hole bigger. For all its ills, Rome had at least kept the nominal churchgoer versed in spiritual things. The Lutherans and Reformed, however, were emphasizing correct doctrine so much that few looked beyond it. The message that came across was, believe the right beliefs and you will be saved. Lifestyle, holiness, and spirituality were largely neglected. One protester accused Luther of "raising up a people altogether callous in sin."[1]

The reaction came quickly. Throughout the German-speaking lands common people sought to go further than Luther had gone. This understandably led to a number of regrettable developments, such as the Peasants' Revolt and the withdrawal of millennialists into idle and often foolish speculation about the second coming. Among orthodox Christians, however, groupings began to form of those who wished simply to live in separation, obedience, and mutual love. The term *Anabaptist* was coined to refer to them. The word suggests rebaptism, and indeed, believer's baptism was usually the common denominator of these various groups, but in many ways the term is unsatisfactory. The groups in question preferred to call themselves "Brethren"—a better title in that it makes the center not a sacrament but the spiritual fruit of love for one another.

As these new churches formed in the early 1520s, one major area of their attention was the practical, material outworking of brotherly love: what to do with goods and possessions. In 1524 the translation of Thomas More's *Utopia* of eight years earlier was published. In it the writer advocates a new social order based on justice and equality:

> To speak plainly my real sentiments, I must freely own that as long as there is any private property, and while money is the standard of all other things, I cannot think that a nation can be governed either justly or happily. . . . I am persuaded that, till property is taken away, . . . the greatest and by far the best part of mankind will still be oppressed with a load of cares and anxieties.[2]

This, along with several editions of the old text of *Piers Plowman*, stressed how all is in common in heaven, and presented community of goods as a vision to be considered. The Anabaptists picked up on this teaching, but with varying stresses. As early as 1523 one Nikolaus Storch was preaching "all things in common" in Saxony. Two years later, Thomas Müntzer, leading light of the Peasants' Revolt, admitted after his arrest that he had planned to introduce communal sharing had the revolt succeeded.

Anabaptism and the Common Life

From the outset there were differences in interpretation of "all things in common." Some Anabaptists chose the Jerusalem model, others the Pauline modifications. The majority of early leaders were of the latter camp. In 1526 Balthaser Hubmaier wrote:

> Concerning community of goods, I have always said that everyone should be concerned for others, so that the hungry might be fed, the thirsty given drink, and the naked clothed, etc. For we are not lords of our possessions, but stewards and distributors. There is certainly no one who says that another's goods may be seized and made common. Rather, he would gladly give the coat in addition to the shirt.[3]

Felix Manz agreed with this interpretation. Georg Blaurock was a little uncertain. When examined, he spoke of "community of all things," but under cross-examination, he admitted that he did not favor common ownership. "He who is a good Christian should share what he has, else he is none."[4]

Twenty-five years later, Menno Simons, founder of the Mennonites, wrote in his *Humble and Christian Justification* in answer to the charge of "communism":

> This accusation is false. . . . We do not teach and practice community of goods but we teach and testify the Word of the Lord, that all true believers in Christ are of one body, partakers of one bread, have one God and one Lord. Seeing then that they are one, it is Christian and reasonable that they also have divine love among them and that one member cares for another, for both the Scriptures and nature teach this. . . . They show mercy and love . . . they have pity on the wants of the saints. They receive the wretched. They take strangers into their houses. They care for the sad. They lend to the needy. They clothe the naked. They share their bread with the hungry.[5]

Menno adds that this way of life has continued, amid cruel persecution and many martyrdoms, for some twenty years, and no widow or orphan has been left to beg. Another leader, Georg Schnabel, has the same interpretation: "Concerning the community of believers and their material goods, we say that everyone willingly helps his poor brother in his need out of his surplus."[6]

Thus, the majority of the Anabaptists rejected property insofar as it was a link to the world and a tool of greed, but accepted it as a means of providing for the poor and loving one another through voluntary donation.

Other Voices

Others, however, still held that goods ought to be held in common. In 1526 a Basel printer produced an edition of the letters of Clement of Rome, including the spurious *Fifth Epistle* on community of goods.[7] This gained even wider circulation when the historian, Sebastian Franck, incorporated it in his *Chronica* of 1531, a most influential Protestant history of the church. Franck thought the epistle to be genuine, and himself believed that private property was a vice. Johannes Eisermann agreed in his 1533 treatise, *On the Common Good.*[8] In 1527 a Nürnberg printer named Johann Hergott was arrested and beheaded for producing a pamphlet in which he said the millennial kingdom was at hand: he foresaw all persons living together in a sort of monastic community, tilling the land and sharing all things in common—both possessions and land—so that the words of the Lord's Prayer, "our . . . our," might be fulfilled.

This belief was technically held by the mainline reformers themselves. Zwingli, in his *Of Divine and Human Righteousness* of 1523, had penned:

> Even if we were not sinful by nature, the sin of having private property would suffice to condemn us before God; for that which he gives us freely, we appropriate to ourselves.[9]

Martin Bucer also held communal sharing to be the ideal state of Christendom. Yet the all-embracing organism that they had founded was in no way able to support such a lifestyle. And the Anabaptists, though keen to break with this hypocrisy, often differed among themselves on how far sharing ought to go. Even among believers in one congregation there could be uncertainty. Of the thirteen couples interrogated at Sorga in Hesse, three held that no Christian should own property, while the remainder advocated ownership tied with liberal giving.

A further complication was the hostility that community of goods aroused in the authorities. It was seen as anarchy and leading to community of wives. Some even feared that it would incite murder and theft, with the rabble crying: "Let's do away with them and seize their goods!" Most Anabaptists, persecuted as they were, certainly did not want to be additionally charged along these lines, so full sharing was largely played down. Anabaptists in the Tirol of Austria advocated community of goods as God's will, but saw that the strict Hapsburg government would never allow it. So they contented themselves with applying it on a household basis.

One brother presents a good example of this. Ambrosius Spittelmaier was imprisoned for his faith in South Germany in 1527, where he was given reams of questions to answer in writing, in the hope that he might trap himself. In his answer he stressed the covenant bond between the brothers and sisters which means that

> we do not want to part from the other at all despite our tensions; none wishes to annoy the other; no one keeps his possessions from the others, but rather all hold everything in common, be they spiritual or material gifts.[10]

Aware of the authorities' touchiness on the subject, he went on to mingle the Jerusalem and the Pauline models:

> A Christian calls nothing his own, not even a place to lay his head. A real Christian should not own more on earth than he

can cover with one foot. This does not mean that he should have no trade, or sleep in the woods, that he should have no fields or pastures, or that he should not work; rather, that he should use nothing for himself alone, saying: "This house is mine, this field is mine, this money is mine." Instead he should say: "Everything is *ours,*" just as we pray: "Our Father." In sum, a Christian should not call anything his own, but hold all things in common with his brother and not allow him to suffer want. I should not work so that my house be filled and my bowl full of meat, but rather I should see that my brother has enough. A Christian is more concerned about his neighbor than about himself.[11]

Spittelmaier also revealed that whenever he met a believer, he would ask him certain questions: whether he was a Christian, how was his life, how he treated his neighbor, and whether he held all things in common with them, so that none suffer want.

Another leader who advocated full sharing, but with caution, was Wolfgang Brandhuber of Linz, who wrote an epistle to the Anabaptists at Rattenberg on the Inn, dated 1529, in which we read:

If God wills it and if the state permits it, all things should be held in common to the greater glory of God, for since we have become partakers of Christ in the greater things (that is, in the power of God), then why not even more so in the least, that is in the material realm? That is not to say that all goods should be piled together, for conditions were not the same in all places. But every head of a household, together with all those living there who are united with him in the faith, should pool their earnings, be they master, servant, maid, wife, or other fellow-believers. Though every worker should be given his daily wages, according to the words of Christ (Matt. 10:10), love should compel each person to put faithfully his wages into the common purse.[12]

Such was the teaching and practice observed in the Tirol, Upper Austria, and parts of Central Germany around the years 1527-35.

The Hutterites

There was one Anabaptist group, however, which went further. In 1528 a group of 250 under Jakob Widemann left the Church at Nikolsburg in Moravia, since they felt it had not gone far enough away from the state church. They wandered toward Austerlitz, laid a cloak on the ground, put all they had on it and vowed to share together in a communism of love for Christ. From these humble beginnings arose the community of the Hutterites, named after their early leader, Jakob Hutter, which was to grow to a membership of around thirty thousand at its peak and which still exists in the United States and Canada.

The major difference with the Hutterites was twofold: (1) for a good while their native Moravia did not oppose them as did the Austrian and German authorities, and the local lords left them to live in peace in large communities; (2) their depth of spirituality led them to a greater awareness of the sinfulness of human nature than most other Anabaptist groups. The interpretations of sharing quoted above (where personal property could be held so long as it was shared) they saw as all right in theory but hopelessly flawed in practice. The deep imprints of the fallen nature on a person's heart meant that self-will and self-love would eventually undermine such a sharing. They saw in full community of goods a vital *discipline* for the Christian, for it dealt a severe blow to self-will. The Hutterites even had a little rhyme to the effect that "communal life would not be hard if there were not such self-regard." They taught that once their hearts had been purged of self-interest through the Holy Spirit and through discipline, true sharing of goods and possessions would flow naturally from them.

One early writer from among them, Ulrich Stadler, wrote in his *Cherished Instructions* of 1537:

> There is one communion of all the faithful in Christ and one community of the holy children called of God.... They have

one mind, opinion, heart and soul ... and alike await one struggle, cross, trial, and, at length, one hope in glory.... Thus in this community everything must proceed equally, all things must be one and communal.... They have yielded themselves and presented themselves to him [Christ] intimately, patiently, of their own free will, to suffer and endure his will.... Therefore they also live together with one another where the Lord assigns them a place, peaceably, united, lovingly, fraternally.

In brief, "one" and "common" build the Lord's house and are pure; but "mine," "thine," "his" and "own" divide the Lord's house and are impure. Therefore, where there is ownership, and one has something, and it is his, and he does not wish to be in common with Christ and his own in life and death, he is outside of Christ and his communion and has no Father in heaven. If he says so, he lies....

For as the sun with its rays is common to all, so also the use of all created things. Whoever appropriates them for himself and encloses them is a thief and steals what is not his. For everything has been created free and in common. Of such thieves the world is full. May God guard his own from them![13]

The Hutterite communities were known as *Haushaben,* where up to a thousand lived together in communal houses. They valued simple dress and food and pursued a large number of crafts and trades. Agriculture was the chief occupation, but pottery, clocks, cutlery, textiles, and even carriages and surgical implements were manufactured. Workmanship was of such high standard that at times their sales rivaled those of Venice. Their workmen were often hired out to local landowners to manage estates or to run mills. Their reliability, skill, and honesty were proverbial.

In education they were far ahead of the world around them, with nursery and school for all the children, who were brought up communally. They also had doctors, whose skills were more than once called upon by their persecutors. (One doctor, Georg

Zobel, was even summoned to Prague in 1581 to treat the emperor.) Hygiene was valued highly, and the devotion to work in the communities meant that health and prosperity grew among them for as long as peace reigned.

In Moravia they were untouched except for short periods, but those in Austria were cruelly harassed, tortured, and killed for their faith and for their communal sharing. The Hutterite *Chronicle*, their massive community diary, lists some 2,200 martyrdoms. There were probably more.

The Hutterites wrote large numbers of treatises and epistles, many of which contain statements on the community of goods. The three main writings were Peter Riedemann's *Account (Rechenschaft)*, a confession of faith; the 1577 *Great Article Book* by Peter Walpot; and the *Chronicle*, written by a number of elders from 1569 onwards. The last of these simply states:

> Christian community of goods was practiced as Christ taught it and lived it with his disciples, and as the first apostolic church practiced it. No one was permitted to be above the others. Those who earlier had been poor or rich now shared one purse, one house, and one table.[14]

Riedemann's *Rechenschaft* of 1540/41 is a deep theological treatise penned in prison as a reasoned account of what the Hutterites believed. Significantly he wrote first of the communion of saints and then of community of goods. The one must come first and lead to the other. "Community," he wrote, "is nothing other than that those who have fellowship have all things in common, none having anything, but each having all things with the other." He saw this as applying first to "the holy things of God," the new life in Christ, and then to material things.

> Now, since all God's gifts, not only spiritual but material, are given to man, not that he should have them for himself but with all his fellows, therefore the communion of saints itself

must show itself not only in spiritual but also in temporal things. . . .

Now, because what is temporal does not belong to us, but is foreign to our true nature, the law commands that none covet foreign possessions (Deut. 5:21). . . . Therefore whosoever will cleave to Christ and follow him must forsake such taking of created things and property (Luke 9:23-26; Matt. 10:32-39). . . . For if a man is to be renewed into the likeness of God, he must put off all that leads him from him, that is, the grasping and drawing to himself of created things. . . . For the more man cleaves to created things and ascribes such to himself, the further does he show himself to be from the likeness of God and the community of Christ.

For this reason the Holy Spirit also at the beginning of the church began such community right gloriously again, so that "none said that any of the things that he possessed was his own, but they had all things in common" (Acts 2:44, 45). . . . If one should say, it was so nowhere but in Jerusalem, it does not follow that it ought not to be so now. For neither apostles nor church were lacking, but rather the opportunity, manner and time. [15]

The most detailed Hutterite account of community of goods is in the third of the *Five Articles,* which constitute the *Great Article Book* of Peter Walpot, dated 1577. Entitled *Concerning True Surrender and Christian Community of Goods,* it surveys the Old Testament concepts of the Jubilee and the faithful remnant, the words of Jesus, and the practice of the Jerusalem Church, applying each to the life of community now. The following extracts illustrate his conclusions:

The devil doth falsely take possession of what is earthly and temporal for his property. For he saith thus to Christ, when he sheweth him the kingdoms of the world: "All this is mine." Even so do his children, who have this deceitfulness of Belial in their hearts. They take possession of property and possess temporal goods, each for himself. But it should not be so among the children of God, but what God doth lend them they have in common and use for the good of all.

He that liveth in property is false in the confession of his faith. For the Christian Faith stateth a holy Christian church and a community of saints. Now where there is no community of saints, there is likewise no true, sincere Christian church. Therefore all lie who say: "Community is not necessary and is no basis of doctrine," for it is an article of the faith, yea, an institution of Christ and of the Holy Spirit and his teaching. Therefore, just as it is necessary for us to hold to the doctrine of the apostles, to prayer and to the breaking of bread, even so is it necessary for us to hold to community of goods. For community is no light matter, as though the apostles did the same out of capriciousness, but it is divine earnest, and is right and meet for us today as it was at Jerusalem and elsewhere.

It is not to love one's neighbor as oneself when one desireth to have, to keep, and to possess self-interest and property; for love is a bond of perfectness, a golden chain about the temple of God.... For to love one's neighbor as oneself is not a part, not half, but having and enjoying all things in common, for the use of all. Without this it is but Pharisaic, heathen, and pretended love.

Whosoever is unfaithful in what is small, that is, in temporal things, is also unfaithful in what is great. That is, he is unfaithful and good for nothing in spiritual things. For if such a one have not the love to present his goods and possessions to be used in common and equally in community, who will believe that he so loveth the brothers that he could lay down his life for them, as Christ and the apostles teach us?

Therefore "sell all things" is a general command and not just advice given.[16]

Alongside these major texts come a host of lesser writings, which were often never printed but were handed down in manuscript from one generation to the next as the community migrated slowly eastwards over the seventeenth to nineteenth centuries. A reply to a Lutheran opponent, dated 1593, contains the following section:

Christian community of goods is for the purpose of providing for the needy believers, who may be old, sick, crippled and unable to support themselves, so that they be furnished with the necessaries of life the same as the others. But you say there can be no community of goods if such are present—you understand the Christian principle of sharing about as well as a blind man appreciates colors![17]

Other manuscripts say much the same:

Community means nothing other than to have all things in common out of love for our neighbor. Each lays down what he has for general use in the community, since they share all with one another, both joy and suffering.... "Mine" and "thine" have been the cause of all wars and still are today. Both are related to greed.... *Love does not seek its own ends, so it obviously seeks community.*[18]

In 1601 one Hutterite member explained:

With us in Christian fellowship and community of goods, the daily labor of a believer is all a labor of mercy, a work of loving service, faithfulness, and pure charity. All the fruit of the brethren's labor is consecrated to the Lord for the support of the hungry and nourishment of the aged.... Each one is to consecrate himself entirely, with all that he has, to the service of God and his saints.[19]

As the Hutterites came into contact with other Anabaptists, responses varied. Some groups joined them, delighted to find the commitment and sharing for which they had longed. Others were skeptical. Some sought to press the notion of having one's own possessions and giving to others out of one's plenty. Peter Walpot replied on one occasion: "I would have to enquire just how much of it you are using in this way.[20]

Also in answer to the stewardship view, Johannes Hauser wrote in 1606:

By community of goods I understand not that one gives only something of that which is superfluous and keeps the most for himself, as was the case under the law and is today the common

> custom the world over. But the community of goods of which
> we speak means that all that one possesses is surrendered, the
> heart is freed from it, and it is gladly and voluntarily given over,
> as the spirit of the gospel requires and as the saints in Jerusalem
> did.[21]

Sometimes groups were moved to start communities along
Hutterite lines but without Hutterite spirituality. The Polish
Brethren, for instance, started a community near Sandomierz in
1569 and called it Raków. Their aim was to follow the
Jerusalem church. Their leader, Gregory Paul, sought Hutterite
counsel in doing so. But the Polish Brethren were Anti-Trini-
tarian in doctrine and weak in discipline. Eventually, this community failed and the Hutterites had to send them a letter
reproving their lack of order and true surrender to God.

Even among established churches the Hutterites had some
effect. Paul Glock, an imprisoned Hutterite, wrote that several
of the local ministers were now instructing their congregations
that community of goods was technically the highest way.
Nothing, however, was put into practice.

Finally, Elder Andreas Ehrenpreis, in an epistle of 1650,
reiterated the parallel between community and the communion bread and wine originally drawn in the *"Didache"* (see
p. 68 above), concluding:

> Whoever speaks of Christ and of love and yet refuses to hand
> his property over to the community, for the sake of Christ and
> the poor, proves by his actions that he loves the things of the
> world more than Christ.[22]

The Hutterites moved slowly eastward under persecution
until they reached Russia at the end of the eighteenth century.
Here they remained until their pacifist views led to trouble and
they were forced to make the long journey to America in the
1870s. At several points along the way inner decay set in and
the true spirituality that led naturally to sharing lapsed. At two

major points, in the 1680s and the 1820s, community of goods was abandoned. Yet, as soon as love was rekindled, sharing in community was naturally restored. Hundreds of Hutterian Brethren (as they prefer to be known) continue to live on in community today, predominantly in South Dakota and Western Canada. The Hutterian Brethren are thus the longest-lived community group in the nonmonastic line. They are a testimony to the power of love in overcoming self-interest.

Münster

The Hutterites also serve as a good counterbalance to the very different community at Münster, which gave the Anabaptist movement as a whole a bad name and which soured for many people the sharing life of community. In the early 1530s, an Anabaptist preacher named Bernhard Rothmann, who was zealous for a just and true lifestyle in Christ, developed a great following at Münster in Westphalia. He taught full sharing in community, as his *Restitution* of 1534 shows:

> Not only have we . . . turned our goods and possessions over to the deacons as communal property and live on it according to our need, but we also praise God through Christ with one heart and mouth. We are willing to prefer one another with all kinds of services.[23]

When most of the population took to these ideas, the Catholic authorities raised an army and besieged the town.

Over the next months, amid famine and bombardment, the inhabitants, under the leadership of two Dutchmen, began to add lunatic practices to the true community of Acts 2 and 4. They crowned a king, proclaimed the kingdom of David, and practiced polygamy while severely condemning adultery. The kingdom, however, was cut short by the eventual sacking of the city and the butchering of its inhabitants.

This unsavory incident proved a convenient weapon for the authorities, who broadcast the details far and wide in an attempt to discredit communal sharing once and for all. The Hutterites joined in the condemnation, calling Münster a "cruel abomination set up and contrived by the devil,"[24] Their own peaceful and wholesome life did little to redress the balance in the minds of most Europeans.

Communitarianism's Bad Press

In England during this period there was less of a communitarian impulse. This was due in part to the dominant personality of Henry VIII and the fact that England was a united monarchy, while Germany consisted of small states and baronies. Henry wanted nothing to shake the political boat. The example of Münster was enough to brand any move toward sharing of goods as revolutionary and a danger to the state. Indeed it was written into the Thirty-Nine Articles of the Church of England (no. 38) that "the riches and goods of Christians are not common, as touching the right, title, and possession of the same, as certain Anabaptists do falsely boast." Though Henry in 1539 relaxed his position somewhat, there was general hostility toward any notion that "all things should be common and nothing severall [held individually]."

Nonetheless in 1549 there arose a movement in East Anglia that advocated social reform and egalitarianism on Christian lines. It became known as Ket's Rebellion after its foremost figure, a prosperous tradesman named Robert Ket. The revolt was by the poorer classes, frustrated beyond endurance by the injustice of their lot. They tore down hedges planted on common land, occupied Norwich (then the second largest city in England), and finally founded a community settlement at nearby Mousehold, where all goods were shared and equality was practiced out of Christian love. This "common welth," as they termed it, was peaceable and efficiently organized. They practiced agriculture and worked in various trades. Townsfolk from Norwich frequently joined their devotions. It was, however, short-lived, for after only a month the Earl of Warwick came against them with an army of mercenaries and killed 3,000 of them.

Mutual Love and Ministry

It has often been supposed that the main thrust of Anabaptism was doctrinal and sacramental. This is partly true, since the baptism and the mass were very much at issue, as was the doctrine of the church. Yet this is to overlook the *love* which characterized the movement as a whole and the Hutterites in particular. They alone restored the fullness of the gospel to the poor and church government to the laity. Roman Catholicism continued to hold to the doctrine of sacerdotalism, namely that the priest alone carries the power of the Holy Spirit and the ability to bring spiritual blessing to others. Even among the Protestants, which claimed the "priesthood of believers," this notion remained implicit. Rome saw the priest as commissioned in apostolic succession from St. Peter, while Protestants regarded their pastor as somehow special through his theological training. Only the Anabaptists resurrected in fullness the scriptural concept of all believers having ministry for the upbuilding of the church (Col. 2:19; 1 Cor. 12:4-31). Many of them saw the highest outworking of this as lying in the sharing of goods and possessions in community.

Chapter 8

The Seventeenth
and Eighteenth Centuries

As the dust of Reformation and Counter-Reformation settled, a definite picture began to emerge. Doctrine had been
tightened, certain abuses corrected, and some superstitions
thrown out, but there was a definite air of conservatism.
Reform could go so far, but no further. One step beyond a
certain limit was to incur suspicion of being a dreaded
Anabaptist. Both Catholics and mainline Protestants shied
away from any issue which might lay them open to the new
charge of "enthusiasm." An enthusiast was held to be some
madcap idealist who thought he had instruction from on high
to reform the church. As such, the term became a useful brake
to apply to any movement which sought to revivify a church
that was growing lukewarm.

Self-interest: A Legacy of the Reformation

The result of this conservative stance was that self-interest,
largely unchecked, ran riot in Christendom. (Those Marxist
critics who see in Protestantism the start of the bourgeois profit-
drive have a point.) The Anabaptists at Münster were enough
to convince the average churchgoer that community and sharing were dangerous. The notion of keeping your possessions
and being ready to distribute should the need ever arise
(whether or not it ever did) was infinitely preferable to human
nature.

The Puritan Richard Baxter lamented that there could be
few scriptural texts more abused than 1 Timothy 5:8: "If any
one does not provide for his own, and especially for his family,
he has disowned the faith." Baxter comments:

> This is made a pretence for gathering up portions and provid-
> ing full estates for posterity, when the apostle speaketh only
> against them that did cast their poor kindred and family on the
> church, to be maintained out of the common stock, when they
> were able to do it themselves.[1]

He could have added that in the very next chapter of 1
Timothy (6:6-10, 17-19) Paul inveighs against riches, the love
of money, and those who keep their wealth instead of being
"liberal" (the Greek root is *koinos*, i.e., having it in common).

Nevertheless there were certain groups which sought to
return to the scriptural patterns of church life. The Brownists
and Baptists in England and the Collegiants of Holland
reinstated believer's baptism and were sorely opposed for it.
The Society of Friends (Quakers) stressed the fear of God, holiness, and the direct, personal inspiration of the Holy Spirit,
which made them prime targets for the campaigners against
"enthusiasm." All these groups attracted a considerable following among those who could see through the shallowness of established church ways. None of them, however, laid emphasis
on separation from the world and on community sharing.
(William Penn, the Quaker leader, actively urged one communitarian group to disband and get out into the world.)
Instead, they preferred the concept of personal stewardship
and freewill offering.

Peter Cornelisz Plockhoy

Communitarian initiatives continued to be put forward by
politicians and social reformers along the lines of More's
Utopia. Foremost among these was a Dutchman, Peter Corne-
lisz Plockhoy, who under the pseudonym Peter Cornelius wrote
several letters to the English parliament and to Cromwell during the Protectorate, advocating social reform and the eradica-
tion of injustice. "Give ear to the poor, for the cry of them is ex-

ceeding great in these nations,"[2] was his rallying cry. He proposed a united religious society made up of small groupings run on extended family lines, sharing all goods, labors, and benefits. The whole would be spiritually ecumenical, a "community of true Christians." Each settlement would center around a hall for common devotions, discussion, and recreation. Only in such a way, Plockhoy argued, could Satan's grip be loosed from the nation.

In a slight modification, he did allow individuals, under certain circumstances, to steward their own goods, but the ideal was a full sharing in community. Anyone wishing to leave would receive back what he had put in, plus a share in any profits made by the society. Motivating the whole were to be "righteousnesse, love, and brotherly sociablenesse, which are scarce anywhere to be found."[3] Jesus was to be the example:

> How far doth Christ excell all others in love, who by his doctrine and example hath instituted a partnership or Society of mutuall love; by the denomination of Brethren; by Abollishing amongst his disciples all preheminency, or domineering of one over another, requiring that the gifts and meanes of sustinance in the world (for necessity and delight) should be Common; having called his people to a moderation, and to a life suitable to pure nature, so that all Christendome ought to be meerly a certain great fraternity consisting of such as (having denyed the world and their own lustes) conspire together in Christ, the sole head and spring of love; doing well to one another, and for his sake distribute their goodes to those that stand in need.[4]

Needless to say, however, such sweeping idealistic reforms made little impression on Cromwell. Plockhoy was left to turn his attention to the New World and draw up plans for a cooperative colony in New Netherland, the modern Delaware.[5]

The Bartholomites

There were, however, several churches over this period which felt led to live a truly communitarian life for Christ.

Some were Catholic in doctrine, others Protestant. But what they shared was a disgust at the prevailing self-centeredness and fear of radicalism in the established church. Among Catholics, the many bands of missionaries who traveled to new areas usually held all in common. This, however, was no permanent foundation, since they were always on the move.

More deliberate was a community founded at Tittmoning, near Salzburg in Austria, with the cumbersome title of the "Institute of Second Order Clergy Living in Community"—more conveniently known as Bartholomites. The founder, Bartholomew Holzhauser, went there in 1640 and determined to introduce the sharing life of the early church among the parish clergy of Salzburg. He won the support of several colleagues, so communal living began. A constitution was drawn up, stressing the sharing of all income and the life in common as the main character of the foundation. All members worked in the normal manner as parish priests. There was no vow, but a look at the constitution reveals that Holzhauser was seeking to introduce the monastic ideal into the world of parish clergy.

The founder died in 1658, but the Bartholomites grew and spread, until by 1685 they had houses in Italy, Poland, Spain, and Germany, numbering some 1,500 members. A gradual mistrust among bishops set in, however, and increasing restrictions were placed upon the Bartholomites. Many finally left and the last house, at Ingolstadt, was suppressed in 1804.

The name and work of Holzhauser continued to be respected, however. In the nineteenth century, when communal living was coming under careful scrutiny, various Catholic churchmen proposed the foundation of community houses run on the lines of Holzhauser's constitution.[6]

Phat Diem

Longer lasting was the community founded by missionaries in the province of Tonkin, China, in 1675. It was called Phat

Diem (House of God) and comprised European and Chinese living in communal harmony together, sharing their possessions and income. All who sought to join signed a written covenant agreeing to live this way. It was pastored by Catholic clergy. Visitors came in large numbers and were struck by the atmosphere of peace and love that prevailed. One bishop, who stayed at Phat Diem for a while in 1850, wrote:

> Here all is in common between European missionaries and Chinese pastors. The community is the mother of all and must give help to those in need and ensure that all receive what they need; all the members are her children and must help her with their various labours.[7]

Community living continued at Phat Diem for nearly 300 years until the Bamboo Curtain fell in the twentieth century.

The Holy Experiment

In the seventeenth century, South America witnessed the rise of a community numbering some 140,000. For all the cynicism of Voltaire and others, recent scholars of the "Holy Experiment" are discovering that it was more genuine and commendable than had been thought. Appalled at the vice, greed, and brutality of the Spanish colonists in their exploitation of the Indians, the Jesuits set up a native society among the Chiquito and Guarani Indians of Paraguay, run as a Christian community.

In each settlement everything was held in common, and life centered around church meetings and communal labor. Everyone tilled the community fields and in return received all they needed. Horses and oxen were likewise shared and the produce stored in common granaries. In addition, handicrafts, weaving, joinery, bell foundry, and even watchmaking were plied in communal workshops. Money was taboo and all outside trade was carried on by barter. The community's own

"Paraguay tea" was a popular currency. Surpluses were used to care for orphans, the elderly, and the infirm, as well as to cover the building of new properties.

Widows and their families lived together in "widows' houses" and were cared for communally. They were seamstresses and made a new suit of clothes for each community member once a year. Visitors were received warmly and lodged in special hospices. They spoke with astonishment of the industry and joyful piety of the members, who, they record, were always playing music in this "jungle Utopia," as it came to be known. The Jesuit missionaries took no profit from the enterprise and even gained a ruling from the king to the effect that all profits should be used for the improvement of communal facilities. The administrative work was all done by Indians. Finally, however, the community fell foul of the greed of the colonists, who convinced themselves that there was gold on the community's land. So troops moved in and the "Holy Experiment" came to an abrupt end.

The Labadists

Among Protestant community movements was that of the Labadists. Jean de Labadie, a Frenchman from near Bordeaux, spent almost his whole life searching for the true way of serving God in the church. He began life as a Jesuit, but left their order in 1639. Then he passed through various of the Catholic orders, preaching social righteousness, new birth, and separation from the world. He seems also to have received the kind of visions and inspirations usually associated with the present-day charismatic movement. Wherever he went he opened his home to others to live with him as a little community, but as yet he did not see this as binding on the whole church. His stand nevertheless brought him much persecution and his life was regularly in danger.

Finally, feeling that no true renewal was possible in the

Roman Church, Labadie became a Calvinist in 1650. First in France, then at Geneva, and finally in the French church in Holland, he sought to bring new life into the Reformed church through practical discipleship, Bible study, house meetings, and much else that was novel for its day. A powerful and magnetic preacher, he once delivered a series of fifty sermons on the theme of repentance. When he felt that they were being insufficiently heeded, he went over them all again! All the while he was coming to see the need for the true church to be a body of regenerate believers who share a new life together— spiritually and materially—in separation from the world. This development in his thought can be traced through his numerous writings over this period.[8]

At length, in 1669, Labadie broke away from all established denominations and began a Christian community at Amsterdam. He was 59 years of age. In three adjoining houses lived a core of some sixty believers, sharing all things. Children were tutored in the home, a printing press was set up, and one of the men operated as a bookseller. Women practiced needlework and performed domestic duties. Persecution forced them to leave after only a year, and they moved to Herford in Germany. Here the community became more firmly established. Several reports are in existence from visitors at that time, who usually came with reservations and mistrust but left convinced that the spirit was genuine. One such visitor was Sophie of Hannover, mother of King George I of England. To this ▪period also date certain miraculous happenings such as healings and spiritual song. A tree that had been chopped down three years previously suddenly burst into leaf when the Labadists arrived.

War forced them to move to Denmark, where Labadie died (1674). His followers returned to Holland, where they set up a community in a stately home—Walta Castle—at Wieuwerd in Friesland, which belonged to three of the sisters. Here printing and many other occupations continued, including farming and milling. One brother, Hendrik van Deventer, skilled in chemistry and medicine, set up a laboratory at the house and treated many people, including the King of Denmark. He is now remembered as one of Holland's first obstetricians.

Anna Maria van Schurman was noted in her day as "The Star of Utrecht" and admired by princes and poets alike for her talents. She spoke and wrote five languages, produced an Ethiopic dictionary, played several instruments, engraved glass, painted, embroidered, and wrote poetry. At the age of 62 she gave up everything and joined the Labadists.

Visitors came from England, Italy, Poland, and elsewhere, but not all approved of the strict discipline. Those of arrogant disposition were given the most menial of jobs. Fussiness in matters of food was overcome since all were expected to eat what was put in front of them. Many did join, however, including Madame Merian, the noted entomological artist, whose *Insect Life of Surinam* became something of a classic. Several Reformed pastors left their parishes to live in community at Wieuwerd. At its peak, the community numbered around 600 with thousands of adherents further afield.

Daughter communities were set up in the New World. La Providence, a daughter community on the Commewijne River in Surinam, proved to be a disaster. The Labadists were unable to cope with jungle diseases and the unresponsiveness of the soil. Moreover, supplies from Holland were regularly intercepted by pirates. More successful was the settlement on Bohemia Manor in Maryland which grew rapidly to some 200 members.

A gradual decline set in in the 1690s and finally the practice of communal sharing was suspended. From that moment on, the Labadists dwindled, both in Friesland and Maryland, until by 1730 both settlements had died out. In their heyday, however, the Labadists had moved in spiritual vigor and love, which kept the community strong.

William Penn, the Quaker leader, records in his journal a

meeting with the Labadists in 1677, which gives an insight into the reasons why these people chose to live a communal lifestyle. Labadie's widow, Lucia, gave her testimony. In her younger days she had mourned the insipid state of the Christianity which she saw around her:

> If God would make known to me his way, I would trample upon all the pride and glory of the world. . . . O the pride, O the lusts, O the vain pleasures in which Christians live! Can this be the way to Heaven?. . . Are these the followers of Christ? O God, where is thy little flock? Where is thy little family, that will live entirely to thee, that will follow thee? Make me one of that number.[9]

Hearing the word of the kingdom of God preached by Labadie, she was convinced of her need to be joined in community living with her fellow believers.

> I resolved, by the grace of God, to abandon all the glory and pride of this world [she had been a noblewoman and heiress to a considerable estate], to be one of those that should sit down with him in a separation from the vain and dead worships of this world. I count myself blessed that ever I met with him, and these pastors, who seek not themselves but the Lord. And we are a family that live together in love—of one soul, and one spirit, entirely given up to serve the Lord; and this is the greatest joy in the world.[10]

Labadie's spirituality, but not his communitarian separation, was paralleled in the Pietist movement in Germany. Many of its leaders, such as Schütz, Spener, and von Merlau, approved Labadie's stance but preferred for their own part to trust in the established structures. Some Pietist community enterprises did, however, arise. The saintly August Francke, professor at Halle University, founded there an orphanage (the "Waisenhaus") in 1696, to be run along Christian communitarian lines, with full equality and sharing of goods. This caused a stir and was famed abroad. Its example inspired in George Whitefield himself a yearning for a similar foundation which eventually saw the light in America.

The Moravians

Another Pietist preacher, Christian David, advocated separation from the world and gathered a fair following. Persecuted for their stance, they were offered refuge by a nobleman, Count Nicholas Zinzendorf, on his estates in Saxony. Here, on a hill called Hutberg (lit., Watch Hill) a settlement was begun, which was named Herrnhut, (The Lord's Watch). Zinzendorf, a dedicated believer, actively supported the move, and it soon became known that persecuted religious groups who wished to live a quiet and godly life, would be welcome at Herrnhut.

Needless to say, a motley collection gathered: Catholics, Pietists, Schwenckfelders, and remnants of the earlier community at Kunwald in Bohemia (see above). There were immediate frictions over doctrine, and the work threatened to end in disaster. Yet God had other plans. On August 13, 1727 (a memorable date to all Moravians), at a Communion service in the church at nearby Bertelsdorf, the Holy Spirit fell in a powerful way, bringing unity, brotherly love, and a deep joy. This experience influenced the life of Herrnhut, and all the members gladly supplied the needs of one another out of their own funds. As yet there was no idea of a common purse, but Zinzendorf repeatedly outlined the principle that each should contribute out of his abundance for the well-being of his brother and sister.

In these early days, most of the property of Herrnhut was in private hands or, as with the pharmacy and the inn, were part of Zinzendorf's own family estate. Gradually, however, moves were made toward common ownership. It was recorded in Herrnhut's diary that in April 1731 several of the younger men had been urged to renounce property and live in community of goods. In January 1733 deaconess Anna Nitschmann and thirteen others moved into a house where they shared everything in common, but she records that suspicion set in and the practice had to stop. Two months later, eight young men vowed to share all in community under the guidance of a brother named Leupold. It seems, however, that these were the few who were considered able and fit to live this way. Others grumbled because they were not allowed to live in such a fashion, though they wanted to. The experimentation trickled on. In 1740 a cloth factory shared its profits communally. A little later one of the "choir houses" for single men introduced a common purse. Both, however, foundered through mismanagement.

The problem was that Zinzendorf himself, the effective leader of the Herrnhuters, or Moravians, as they were known, had an ambivalent attitude toward communal sharing. He repeatedly said it was not for everyone, that it led to enthusiasm, that the Jerusalem Church was not a blueprint for all time, and that the reality was the mystical body. At the same time, however, he stressed that it was right for all true disciples to renounce worldly property and put it all at the disposal of one's brothers and sisters. This Zinzendorf did with his own income.

By 1748 proposals were being made to take bakeries and slaughterhouses out of private hands and to put them into common ownership. Bakers were making a healthy profit while others had to be maintained from the poor fund. This, coupled with the fact that the church itself had debts of 3,500 *Taler* (a considerable amount) led to a practical solution which was, in essence, a neat compromise. Each member was entitled to retain his goods and contribute as needed, while the businesses were to be communally owned and staffed, with profits used to the advantage of all members alike—a mixture of stewardship and the common purse. It succeeded and debts were canceled. Indeed the businesses did so well that profits soon abounded.

Zinzendorf saw nothing wrong in this, declaring that it was an integral part of making one's sister and brother rich.

The fullest outworking of community of goods among the Moravians was in America. In 1734 the first immigrants landed. Over the next years they established settlements called Bethlehem and Nazareth in Pennsylvania. Their bishop, August Spangenberg, drew up with help from Zinzendorf a social plan called the General Economy. The inspiration for this came from the life of common sharing which Moravians had had to adopt during the Atlantic crossings. It resulted in a system whereby all lesser, personal items were stewarded by individual members, but anything larger was used communally. All capital was deposited without interest in the General Economy, to be used by the community until the depositor chose to withdraw it again. The aim was to be fully self-supporting and independent. After eighteen years, however, Indian raids and massacres, with ensuing financial loss, led to the annulling of the Economy in 1762.

The Moravians were vigorously evangelistic and conceived the vision of establishing a series of "settlements" (or self-sufficient church-villages) throughout Europe and America. Sometimes community of goods was practiced from the outset until a settlement was fully operational, when the dual financial pattern took over. Soon Moravians found themselves missioning over large areas of the globe. In South Africa in the nineteenth century they could boast of one community at Gnadenthal where 1,276 Hottentots lived in harmony with a few Europeans in 276 cottages. There they shared the labor, cared for the poor and widowed, and kept separate from the world.

In England the first settlement was in Yorkshire in 1748 and was named Fulneck after a place in Moravia. Houses, a school, a farm, a shoemaker's shop, a tailor's shop, a glove factory, and a clothing business served the several hundred Moravians as well as the neighborhood. They also made a much-prized paper with a marble effect. They even traded with Portugal and Russia. All profits from their businesses were held in common.

Accommodation was in men's and women's houses, where members slept in dormitories. Their dress was modest. The women wore long dresses with a three-cornered white shawl. They wore different-colored ribbons in their hair to distinguish between the married, single, and minors. This lifestyle led to the usual accusations of immorality with the added suspicion of espionage, since so many members were German. Even where they were accepted (for example by John Wesley), their enclosedness was viewed with suspicion and their industry as wanton profit-making.

They were better received in Ireland, where their community, called Gracehill, endeared itself to the people so that it escaped pillage in the 1798 rebellion.

A third community called Fairfield near Droylsden (founded 1785), manufactured cotton and became a center for Moravian supplies when a canal was dug past it. It also boasted a trombone band.

Decline set in during the nineteenth century among the English communities. One by one factories were sold, and what had previously been shared was apportioned out. Only the schools continued in a healthy state. Today the Moravians are still best known for their missions. Recent historians have tended to stress missions so much that they have overlooked basis for such outreach: sharing in love. Although this was not a full sharing in a common purse, it was an expression of the common life in a twofold form, stewardship *and* common sharing, which has served as a model for subsequent community groups down the years.

The Trevecka Family

England at this time was fertile ground for community. The age of Walpole knew corruption of justice, press-gangs, an epidemic of gin drinking, and misery among the poor. This scene is well captured in the engravings of Hogarth and in the popular "Beggar's Opera." Church attendances were bolstered by imposing fines for absence, but when the king offered an indulgence on the point, large numbers broke off churchgoing altogether. Irreligion was entrenched in rural parts and whole villages were without the good news of the gospel.

In this scene rose Whitefield, Wesley, Rowland, and many others who fearlessly brought the Word of God to rich and poor alike, amid scenes of fierce persecution. Wesley battled for years to remain within the Church of England, but finally felt forced to withdraw. His societies of regenerate believers were a powerful force, since they stood as a visible alternative to the self-centeredness and depravity of normal life.

Wesley himself never approved of "all things in common," but one of the other leaders of the revival did. Howell Harris, a fiery Welshman, was an inspired orator and gifted evangelist. It was he who led George Whitefield into open-air preaching. He traveled widely, laboring tirelessly in the gospel amid severe opposition, beatings, and arrests, and through him hundreds were won to Christ. The strain, however, began to tell upon his constitution. In 1751 he experienced a physical and possibly a nervous breakdown. He withdrew to his family village of Trevecka in Brecknockshire, Wales, sorely afflicted within and without. He was effectively confined to his bedroom for two years. To his surprise, many families of believers loyal to him traveled to Trevecka to be with him. The buildings were insufficient to handle the new influx, so the old house was pulled down and a new one started. The new house was to be the home of a Christian community known as "The Trevecka Family."

Some unkind scholars have pointed to the fact that Harris began community living when not wholly in control of himself. But this overlooks two things. First, some years before, Harris had been fired by the example of the Pietists at Halle who had founded an orphan house served by a Christian community. He had on several occasions spoken of his desire to do the same one day. Second, Harris recovered from his illness after some two years, yet did not plunge back into an itinerant ministry. Instead, he spent the rest of his life building up the "Family" and shepherding its members, stressing in interviews and letters that this was the desire of his heart.

Harris's vision is clearly portrayed in the following letter:

> He [God] allways gathered His followers together in little Companies where He reveals His glory and manifests Himself. These congregated Societies are ye City on a Hill, ye Garden, ye Vineyard, ye Churches.'[11]

This he sought to establish at Trevecka. He corresponded with Zinzendorf and his followers and paid a visit to the Moravians at Fulneck to learn from their experience. The new house and outbuildings were constructed around gardens where members could walk and pray. There were barns, coach houses, a woolen mill, a tucking mill, a printing press, and a chapel. The great house itself had many dormitories and rooms. Its exterior was ornately decorated. The great hymn writer, William Williams, sang the beauty of this "castellated monastery." John Wesley wrote in 1763:

> Howell Harris' house is one of the most elegant little places which I have seen in Wales. The little chapel, and all things round about it, are finished in uncommon taste, and the gardens, orchards, fishponds, and the mount adjoining, make the place a little paradise. He thanks God for these things and sees through them [i.e., sees God in everything and does not glory in the human achievement]. About six score people are now in the Family, all diligent, all constantly employed, all fearing God and working righteousness.[12]

Wesley was eager, however, to urge them to witness and not to be withdrawn.

Goods and income were shared at Trevecka and all members worked for the "Family." Hannah Bowen, as matron, supervised the house. Each woman had clearly defined domestic duties, spun flax, or wove cloth. The men practiced various trades: pottery, printing, bookbinding, cobbling, tailoring, carpentry, and gardening. There was a blacksmith, a currier, a sawyer, a tiler, a master mason, a coachman, and an ostler. Farming was the main occupation. The community owned or rented several farms. Livestock was raised for meat and dairy products. Trevecka was one of the first farms in Wales to practice crop rotation in the modern sense and to grow turnips for fodder. Buying goods was in the hand of an estate manager, James Pritchard.

For the first few years financial strain was acute, but finally debts were paid and life became quiet and trouble free. Visitors came in droves. They were fed and lodged on the condition that they join in the daily work. Harris used to tell them that they were welcome to stay a few days, after which they could remain if they "found ye Saviour." Those who did not, had to leave, "for this is not an ale-house." Other leaders of the revival would also stay from time to time.

Life was disciplined in the Family. Members rose around 5:00 a.m. for a brief sermon from one of several brothers called exhorters. After breakfast they worked until lunch at noon. In the afternoon while work continued, visitors were received for a special address in English and Welsh. At the evening meal Harris would examine the elders as to their life and growth, after which there was a sermon and time for informal fellowship before bed.

Members were free to leave the community whenever they chose. Some did—usually to get married, since celibacy was prized at Trevecka.

Between 1770 and 1805 more than 100 books were printed at Trevecka. The trades and crafts practiced led Harris to claim that they corresponded to 70 trades in London. Blind and crippled people were taken in and cared for. An outbreak of smallpox decimated the population, but new members continued to join. After Harris's death in 1773 the leadership passed to Evan Moses, supported by several elders. A gradual dwindling in numbers ensued, since no one seemed to recapture the prophetic presence of Harris. By 1830 the community had largely dispersed.

In its heyday (c. 1759-1775), the Trevecka Family was a force to be reckoned with. The Wesleys praised it, locals overcame their suspicions and valued its presence, and its workers were much sought after because of their diligence and honesty. One employer wrote to Harris: "I want a person of real skill, knowledge and honesty, and from your general character I can apply nowhere so properly as to you." Another added: "Their conduct does credit to the religious principles you have taken so much pains to instil in them."[13] In Wales the subsequent decline is often overlooked today and affection is still expressed for Howell Harris's "Family."

The Ephrata Cloisters

Meanwhile in America, a man named Conrad Beissel was searching for Christian reality. A native of Baden, Germany, he was converted in 1717 and three years later emigrated to America. By all accounts a man of lively intelligence, great energy, and inspiring eloquence, he went to Germantown, Pennsylvania, and worked as a weaver. Discontented with this, he tried the life of a hermit. Then he pastored a Baptist-style church. Yet his longing was for a true sharing in brotherly love. Finally, in 1732, Beissel founded a community in Lancaster County, Pennsylvania, and called it Ephrata, after the ancient name for Bethlehem.

Log huts were erected and brothers and sisters lived segregated, sharing all things in common. Numbers grew to some 300. As trade brought fresh funds, the huts were demolished and houses built, in the German style, with high, steep roofs and many little rooms of about six by nine feet. Also built were a paper mill, a flour mill, an oil press, a bakery, a school, a printing office, an almonry, and several shops.

Marriage and celibacy were both accepted at Ephrata. Some chose to stay celibate in almost a monastic way, shaving a part of their head as a sign. Worship was conducted in a large hall and involved much music. It has been claimed that America's first singing school was at Ephrata, and indeed, many visitors' accounts testify to the beauty and artistry of the singing.

The story is told of how some envoys from the English government were so struck by the music that they sent some of the community's sheet music to the royal family who replied by sending a gift in a box. Only Beissel and the estate manager ever saw the gift, however, for the box was promptly buried in a secret place, lest it foster pride in the community.

Beissel was adamant that riches should not be a part of community life, so profits from the businesses were used to repair the residential premises. When Governor Penn offered him 5,000 more acres, Beissel declined, believing that it would be injurious to their spiritual life to accumulate property.[14]

Visitors came in droves to Ephrata, not least to gape at its massive buildings, unique in the United States. Some also joined the community, but its numbers never reached more than about 300. By 1920 it had effectively ended, after nearly 200 years. Perhaps the best known tribute to the community's life was that given by soldiers of the American army in the War of Independence, who took over one of the community's buildings as a hospital and were full of admiration for the patient and sacrificial service of the sisters.

The Amish

Another community which deserves mention here is that of the Amish. They arose from a division in the Swiss Anabaptist-

Mennonite movement in the last decade of the seventeenth century, believing that the existing group had slipped in areas of discipline. Several hundred broke away under the leadership of an elder named Jakob Ammann and sought to return to the foundational creed of the Mennonites. They were numerous at first in Alsace, France, but gradually migrated to the New World over a period of a century. There are now some 20,000 Amish in the United States and Canada.

The Amish have become something of a sociologist's dream nowadays, since they practice rigorous separation from the world and mistrust all modern inventions, which they see as potentially dangerous to spirituality. Consequently, dress is simple, old-fashioned and often black—the men with beards, hats, and braces, the women with head coverings. Electric lighting is generally not tolerated. In some groups mechanized agricultural machines are now allowed, but their bishops still do not allow them to own automobiles. The Amish use horses and travel in carriages. Education is kept to a minimum, for labor on the land is seen as a better and purer way.[15]

The important distinctives of Amish life may be summed up as follows: (1) separation from the world; (2) the vow of obedience, following baptism; (3) an ordered and disciplined lifestyle, with an authority structure and a code of practice; and (4) a strict church discipline to cope with backsliders and rebels. In theory there is no doctrine of sharing goods and possessions in common—they hold to the stewardship pattern. But in reality, the fact that their settlements are utterly exclusive means that sharing happens. And it works. There is a written rule known as the "Aid Plan" whereby all members undertake to compensate anyone who loses property by fire or storm. (This is seen as preferable to the world's insurance companies.) Whenever a member needs to build a house or barn, the whole local community contributes liberally with the finance and labor required to build it.

Chapter 9
The Nineteenth Century

The nineteenth century produced political and social conditions that were fertile for the growth of communities. Napoleon had criss-crossed Europe with new roads and building projects as he sought to build a massive empire. His exploits left the common person with an appreciation for the small things in life. Modernization was resisted and tradition upheld.

On the spiritual front, the church was subjected to an unprecedented barrage as humanistic and scientific trends drew the bulk of nominal churchgoers after them. Many diverse leaders and movements combined to shake the faith to the core—Darwin and evolution; Freud and psychoanalysis; Marx with his plans for a whole new sociopolitical order without religion; and theologians applying human reason to undermine almost everything of faith and spirituality.

As a result, many Christians withdrew into themselves, holding a personal faith but largely keeping quiet about it in an increasingly hostile climate. Others—not only Christians—felt a strong call to community. The apparent failure of accepted forms of government led many to see the answer in what they called "cooperatives," which were communities based on the abolition of private property and the provision of work for all for the common good. They had behind them the rallying cry of 1789, "Liberty, Equality, and Fraternity!" and the words of Rousseau, "Between two united hearts, community of goods is a necessity and a duty."

Robert Owen, the father of modern socialism, was foremost with these ideas. He wrote voluminously and founded the London Cooperative Society. The French theorists had similar plans, now known as Saint-Simonist, Fourierist, or Icarian, after their inspirers.

All these founded communities, mostly in America. They soon found, however, that they did not work. The very self-assertion and greed which they were designed to overcome proved their undoing. There was no foundation of a changed heart through the converting work of God. The result was something of a mockery, as can be judged from a contemporary satirical verse:

> What is a Communist? He that has yearnings
> For equal division of unequal earnings.
> Idler or bungler, or both, he is willing
> To fork out his penny and pocket your shilling.[1]

The Harmony Society

Yet there were several communities founded at this period out of a true Christian love and obedience to the commands of Scripture. Here again, though the theory had come from Europe, the practice was in America. In 1803 a group emigrated from Württemberg to Pennsylvania under the leadership of Johann Georg Rapp (1757-1847), a linen weaver who had separated from Lutheranism. Rapp held to adult baptism, a simple biblicism, and the need for separation from the spirit of the world. He was outspokenly critical of the world's social system and its inherent selfishness.

In 1804 he founded a community north of Pittsburgh and called it Harmony. Six hundred or so vowed to share their possessions, till the land, and live in simple devotion to God and one another. A constitution of 1805 amounted to a covenant vow of submission and the community of goods. The common fund of the Harmony Society was to be managed by trustees for the good of all. Anyone leaving could receive back the value, without interest, of what he or she had donated. (Subsequently this clause was repealed as being out of keeping with a true spirit of giving.)

Although there was some turbulence and loss of members, there were still 450 when the community moved to Indiana in 1815. Here they set about building mills, factories, and farms.[2] Their success was such that their prosperity grew, but all profits were used to improve common facilities. One visitor at this time wrote:

> They have made the "wilderness to bloom as the rose." They have done more essential good for this country in the short period of five years than the same number of families scattered about the country have done in fifty. And this arises from their unity and brotherly love . . . they know no mercenary view, no self-interest, except that which adds to the interest and happiness of the whole community. . . . Sometimes nearly the whole force of the Society, male and female, is directed to one object, such as pulling flax, reaping, hoeing corn, etc., so that the labor of a hundred acre field is accomplished in a day or two. All, in fact, seems to go on like clockwork, and all seem contented and happy.[3]

Georg Rapp (he dropped his first name) was, by all accounts, a strong-willed but sensitive man, devoted to the service of the flock. He was supported by several elders, one of whom wrote to an inquirer in 1823:

> The Society is prospering externally and internally. We live in peace and unity, which gradually binds us faster and faster into one body, whereof one member renders to another the necessary assistance, which facilitates the toils of life in great measure.[4]

By this time the Harmony Society had gained worldwide attention. The English poet Byron wrote about it in his *Don Juan* (Canto 15, strophes 35-38); economists and social reformers looked to it as a model; princes and politicians visited and were profoundly impressed.[5] When it seemed right to Rapp and his associates to sell the community's site on the Wabash River in

Indiana, it was bought in 1825 by Robert Owen who founded "New Harmony." This attempt at community living on moral lines ended, however, in failure.

The daily pattern at Harmony was to rise at six and work until six in the evening, eating at nine and twelve. Meals were not rushed, since they were regarded as an important expression of unity. There were two meetings on Sundays and two midweek. Evenings were given to relaxed fellowship. Private devotions were encouraged, and there was a three-acre park laid out where members could walk and muse. Children were educated until the age of fourteen, then channeled into such occupation within the community as their talents indicated.

A serious schism occurred when a self-styled "Count de Leon" (in reality a humble Bernhard Müller) joined and proved divisive, not least because he claimed to be the Lion of the Tribe of Judah. When he finally left, he took a third of the membership, some 250, and set up his own colony in 1832. The seceders were repaid a staggering $100,000 from the common fund. Others left in order to get married, not wanting to submit their desire to the common witness of the leadership.

By this time the community had moved back to the Pittsburgh area, where they renamed their community Economy. Here Rapp penned the only real work of devotion to come out of the Harmony Society, *Thoughts on the Destiny of Man* (1824). Here he stresses the "union of harmonious minds" which God intends to operate on earth as part of his reconciliation of all things to himself. Therefore Christian community was a foretaste of the life of heaven. Of life at Economy, Rapp writes:

> In the common household of this brotherhood, the greatest order, diligence. and skill are observed in the most minute, as well as in the most extensive transaction. Here wealth is possessed in abundance, and all cares for sustenance are removed and forgotten.... Male and female, old and young,

are usefully employed, according to their powers of mind and body; all contribute to the welfare of the whole, and from the common stock every individual is supplied.... The various branches of this economic commonwealth, thus regularly conducted and united together, form one great machine . . . for the common interest of the whole. In their mutual enjoyments all the members are contented and happy; none are rich or poor; the causes of distress and clamour in the world are not experienced, nor even known here.[6]

The exodus of members, coupled with increasing financial pressures bred of the devaluation of paper money, put the community under great stress in the ensuing years. After the death of elder Jacob Henrici in 1897, it was decided to dissolve the common fund—a move which officially took place the following year. Harmonists continued to exist, however, in a non-communitarian form. Some former members were taken under the wing of a Hutterian colony in South Dakota, where they were able to continue the sharing life of "all things in common." This, after all, had been the heart and soul of the Harmonists, and is well captured in the following extract from a letter written in 1822 by Rapp's son, Frederick, which also underlines the essential difference between Christian and socialist communities:

Here at Harmony we are all those who have been prepared and fitted for the kingdom of God. Thus it is natural that all private ownership had to be abolished, because in the kingdom of God no one has his own possessions but everything in common. This is why we all have one common interest here; all who are sound members of the body find that brotherly love urges them, voluntarily and uncoerced, to care for the needs and happiness of his brother with zeal and toil, both materially and spiritually.... Without the abolition of ownership no true community can stand, but again and again desire, self-will, and self-interest arise and become an irresistible drive to destruction. This is why all the plans to found communities like Harmony, but without the practice of the faith of Christ and abolition of ownership, have till now foundered.[7]

The Zoar Society

Another group of immigrants from Württemberg arrived in America in 1817. Some 200 people under the leadership of Joseph Bäumeler (or Bimeler) bought land in Tuscarawas County, Ohio, and built a village called Zoar, after the place of Lot's refuge from the destruction of Sodom. At first there had been no thought of sharing in community, but by 1819 circumstances necessitated it and it was found to be fruitful.

Zoar was laid out carefully, with community houses, chapel, shops (where knitwear produced by the sisters was sold, as well as agricultural produce), a blacksmith's shop, a carpenter's shop, a joinery, and a farm. Care was taken to lay out gardens and plant orchards, which led many visitors to remark on the sheer beauty of the settlement. Members pursued trades and crafts, tilled the soil, tended herds of cattle, or were hired out to neighboring farms. In 1827 a canal was planned by the state, running through their land, so the Separatists (as they were known) gained a contract worth $21,000 to do some of the work. The canal brought increased prosperity to Zoar in the course of the years.

Members shared all things in common and gave themselves to celibacy in order to be more devoted to God. In later years marriage was allowed. Bimeler, a man of little education but spiritual and practical prowess, regularly taught on the necessity of doing all for the common good. When he died in 1853, three volumes of his addresses along with devotional fragments gleaned from the community as a whole were published. One elder told a visitor:

> In heaven there is only community; and why should it not be our aim to prepare ourselves in this world for the society we are sure to enter there? If we can get rid of our willfulness and selfishness here, there is so much done for heaven. . . . Charity and genuine love to one another, which are the foundations of true Christianity, can be more readily cultivated and practiced in community than in general, isolated society. A community is

the best place in which to get rid of willfulness, bad habits, and vices generally, for we are subject to the constant surveillance and reproof of others, which, rightly taken, will go far toward preparing us for the great Community above.[8]

In 1832 Zoar was incorporated under Ohio law as the Society of Separatists of Zoar. Its finances were managed by trustees, who also had the spiritual and practical oversight of community affairs. People interested in joining lived in the community and were paid wages for one year to work in the mills. Those still wishing to join became members of the First Class, which carried no right to vote or hold office, and which allowed a refund of contributions should a member leave. Transfer to the Second Class meant a signing of the Covenant and an entire surrender of goods forever. In case of such a member leaving, the trustees would consider a discretionary refund on the basis of how the member had conducted himself. At the time of the incorporation, there were 500 members. By 1874 there were about 300, stewarding property worth over a million dollars.

A decline set in after a cholera epidemic cut members by a third. Zoar was forced to employ outside labor, which had a bad effect on community standards. Many were happy to remain in the First Class and not proceed to "full" membership. Most serious of all was a decline in spiritual inspiration. Meetings consisted of reading Bimeler's addresses; nothing was new and alive; young people grew restless. Several attempts were made through law to have property divided up, though the ruling always went in favor of the community. Finally, in 1898, a voluntary suspension of sharing was introduced, and the community of Zoar, its original heart thus cut out, died a natural death by 1910.

The Amana Society

Back in Germany in 1714, two separatists named Johann Rock and Eberhard Gruber founded a society called the "Community of True Inspiration." This name came from their belief that truly regenerate and committed Christians were directly inspired by the Holy Spirit here and now. They were Pietists in their devotion, believed in true separation from the world, and lived according to Scripture and a set of *Rules for Daily Life* drawn up by Gruber. The following are excerpted from that set of rules:

> 8. Live in love and pity toward your neighbor, do not indulge in anger or impatience of spirit. . . .
> 10. Count every word and thought or work as done in the immediate presence of God. . . .
> 16. Have no dealings with worldly minded men, never seek their society; speak with them little, and never without need.[9]

However, it was not until a century later that the "Inspirationists" gained a distinctive form as a Christian community. Under the leadership of a gifted pastor named Christian Metz (1794-1867), some 600 members emigrated to America. In 1842 they settled near Buffalo in New York County, calling their village Ebenezer. Soon they moved to the state of Iowa, where, in 1855, they founded a communitarian settlement. They called it Amana, after a mountain mentioned in the Song of Solomon (4:8) meaning "remain steadfast." Within a few years it comprised seven villages: Amana, West Amana, South Amana, East Amana, Middle Amana, High Amana, and Homestead, with a total of some 26,000 acres, 10,000 of which were forested.[10]

Farming was the main occupation at Amana, but woolen mills produced a wool of such quality that it was much sought after. There were also a cotton print factory, flour mills, a saw mill, a dye shop, an icehouse, a slaughter house, and a bakery. Members were all employed in these community businesses and were accommodated in shared houses, grouped in quadrangles around a large garden. All ate at one table, served from a common kitchen. Children were educated within the community, but along public school lines, from age six to fourteen, then channeled into one of the businesses. The women also performed domestic duties.

In 1859 the community was incorporated under Iowa law as the Amana Society and drew up a detailed constitution, part of which reads:

> That the foundation of our civil organization is and shall remain forever God, the Lord, and the faith which he worked in us. . . . That the land purchased here, and that may hereafter be purchased, shall be and remain a common estate and property, with all improvements thereupon, as also with all the labor, cares, troubles and burdens, of which each member shall bear his allotted share with a willing heart. Agriculture and the raising of cattle, in connection with some trades, shall under the blessing of God form the means of sustenance of this Society. Out of the income of the land and the other branches of industry the common expenses of the Society shall be defrayed.[11]

Individual members shared all their goods and capital, receiving in return from the common fund according to their needs. This was done on the basis of each family or single member having an annual credit at the community's stores, to which they could go and receive what they required. Profits and surpluses were used to "improve the common estate of the Society." This improvement included new buildings, vehicles, printing, and care of the sick and aged. All was to be governed by elders, of whom there were 70 at the peak of Amana's growth. These elders were in turn led and overseen by Metz himself, who is remembered as a most understanding and compassionate leader, for all his strict discipline.

One nineteenth-century writer on the Amana Society said:

> It is the firm belief of the leaders that religion is the necessary foundation of communism [meant, of course, in the sense of sharing], and that their own communism is simply an out-

> growth of their religious life. The most fundamental thing with them is not communism, but religion. . . . As one of their elders told me, the rock upon which their organization is built is obedience. As the three words which give form and direction to democratic communism are liberty, equality and fraternity, so the three words which express what is most fundamental in this Christian Community are authority, obedience, and fraternity.[12]

The same writer stressed the atmosphere of love which pervaded life both at home and at work in the Amana community.

Amana still exists, but in a very different form. As at Zoar, the spirit of inspiration left the Inspirationists. Where in former days there had been eleven meetings a week, well attended and powerful, services lapsed into a reading of Metz's addresses. This reading was valued by the older members, but had little appeal to the young, who drifted away toward the towns.

By 1930, the time of the depression, Amana had debts of nearly $400,000. Two years later, community sharing was suspended and a new cooperative capitalism began. Each member received one share of the Amana Society businesses, which now produced tourist goods, refrigerators, grandfather clocks, and furniture (and, in the present day, microwave ovens). Outside labor was brought in and trade grew rapidly. Shares eventually multiplied in value thirty times and the community's assets now top $8,000,000.

"Community" has taken on a social rather than religious sense, and the 1,600 Amana members continue as an ethnic German-American group, without the former glory of costly sharing in mutual love. Religious observance is neglected. But older members of the community, who remember the days of "all things in common" before the "Great Change" of 1932, confide to visitors that it has been a change for the worse.

Bethel and Aurora

A comparatively short-lived community foundation was that instituted by William Keil. A native of Prussia (1812), he emigrated to America and operated as a faith healer until converted to Methodism at the age of 30. After a few years he separated from the Methodist Church and was joined by many Germans, including some who had left Amana. In 1844 they purchased 2,500 acres of land in Shelby County, Missouri. Here they founded a settlement called Bethel, where everything was held in common out of love for Christ. At first very poor, the community worked hard on the land and was soon able to build a woolen mill, a gristmill, a sawmill, several shops, and a chapel.

By 1854 there were around 650 members at Bethel, and Keil felt it was time to start a daughter colony. So he and a party of brethren traveled to Oregon, where they founded a community and named it Aurora. Here, too, success was quickly apparent and numbers soon reached 400. All the trades practiced at Bethel were practiced in Aurora, where they also grew and dried fruit.

Until 1872 all property at both communities was registered in Keil's own name. Technically it was apportioned out to each individual member, but in practice it was held and shared together. Any member needing something from the common store made a request, and if genuine need could be demonstrated, he or she received it. In addition, each family was given a number of pigs, cows, and chickens to tend.

Bethel and Aurora were apparently so fully dependent upon the strong leadership of Keil that, when he died in 1877, nobody could fill his place. Life in community dwindled away until by 1884 it no longer existed—after only forty years. One writer at this time nevertheless noted: "Quite a number of the former members regret the dissolution of the communities and regard the years spent in them as the happiest of their lives."[13]

The Common Life in India

Meanwhile in Asia, communitarian developments were in evidence. Anthony Norris Groves, a dentist from Plymouth and one of the early missionaries of the Plymouth Brethren, established a household in Baghdad in the 1830s. Later he began one in India, where all things were shared in common between fellow missionaries and indigenous helpers. It was in this context that he penned in his journal:

> We purpose that our domestic arrangements should all be very simple and very inexpensive, and our plan strictly evangelical. Our great object will be to break down the odious barriers that pride has raised between natives and Europeans ... and I do not yet despair of seeing in India a church arise that shall be a little sanctuary in the cloudy and dark day that is coming on Christendom.[14]

Thirty years later the church in South India was being swept by that great phenomenon of the nineteenth century, a revival. One observer and instrument of the awakening, Henry Groves, wrote of its fruits in the Arulappatoor area:

> There are now in Christian Pettah alone about one hundred who are bound together in the ties of Christian fellowship, and in the district of Arulappatoor there is about the same number. . . . Sunday they make a day of special fasting and prayer, abstaining often from food till after the partaking of the Lord's Supper. . . . They appear to be living in much real simplicity, having all that they have in common, and working together for the common good.[15]

Thus, in a way reminiscent of the church of Acts 2 and 4, Groves linked the purpose of God in revival with community—the sending of the Holy Spirit in power with the joining of the awakened in the sharing bond of true *koinonia*.

The works of Finney, Sprague, and other revivalists reveal the *corporate* nature of that century's revivalism. It was marked by *corporate* prayer and penitence, *corporate* grief over failure, *corporate* seeking after zeal and blessing. However, once revival broke out, its buoyancy often came to be regarded as an end in itself, to be grasped and held by individuals. Falling foul of the sensual excitability of human nature, revival fires often burned themselves out very quickly. Such was a travesty of God's purpose: corporate in its inception, the awakening of godliness was meant to be corporate in its outworking and its fruit.

The Cokelers

In 1850, a shoemaker from London was seeking a church which lived a life of communal separation. His name was John Sirgood. One night he had a dream in which he was told that a certain area of North Sussex would be ready to receive the word of separation and community. He and his wife, unable to afford public transport, duly walked the forty miles from Clapham to Loxwood, near Petworth. Here they were eventually able to buy a cottage, and in it Sirgood preached. Followers were soon gathering regularly on Sundays and midweek.

Basing the name on one of Sirgood's favorite phrases, "dependent on Christ," the church called itself the "Society of Dependents." To the locals, however, their habit of drinking cocoa instead of alcohol gave them the nickname of "Cokelers," by which title they have been known ever since. They held strict separation from the world. Their dress was modest and simple. They shunned tobacco, alcohol, secular music and literature, dancing, theater, and even flowers in the home. Their government was by lay pastors, to whom they referred as "stalwarts." Their faith was marked by holiness and asceticism. Marriage was regarded as second best. Victory over sin was possible to the truly regenerate (in this they follow Wesley's stress on Christian perfection). The church was seen as "a favored people, peculiar to Christ." The Bible was the foundation of their creed, and members were expected to memorize lengthy sections of it.

As the church grew in numbers, houses were bought in several villages, among them the local manor house. Here members lived in community with money and possessions in common. Chapels were set up further afield for their numerous adherents, for example at Chichester, Hove, and Norwood. Persecution was stirred up by the squire and the vicars of local parishes, and for a time it looked as though Sirgood would be expelled. But the Repeal of the Conventicle Act removed the threat, and the Cokelers were free to live their communal life in peace. By 1905 it was estimated that one third of the population of the Weald of Sussex was loyal to the community. A daughter settlement was also started in America.

The community supported itself by farming and commerce. Several shops were opened where foodstuffs, haberdashery, and china were sold. These were cooperative enterprises, owned, financed, and run by the church. Where possible, communal living quarters were set up above the shops and nearby. At one place, Lord's Hill, the building complex became a community village in its own right. These stores ensured a degree of self-sufficiency and a steady revenue. As the years went by, they were joined by other commercial and industrial enterprises: a steam bakery, a bicycle repair shop, and handicraft workshops. At the turn of this century, the community was even able to purchase several automobiles for the transportation of community members to the chapel, some of the first in the county.

Sirgood preached often on the necessity of unity, or as he would call it, "Combination." To him "Combination" was a theological principle of oneness in which rich and poor, strong and weak, old and young combine in Christ to live a separate and radically different lifestyle. One early leader, Henry Aylward, exemplified this by bringing a blind girl to live, work, and be cared for in the community. "Combination" also appears in the Dependants' hymns, one of which speaks of

> Christ's combination stores for me,
> Where I can be so well supplied,
> Where I can one with brethren be,
> Where competition is defied.[16]

When John Sirgood died in 1885, the community numbered around 2,000. Chapels were located in a dozen places and stores in seven or eight. Its members were predominantly "the poor of this world": artisans, farm laborers, and serving maids. In thirty-five years they had become respected for their enterprise and their godliness. Even the vicars who previously persecuted them now spoke in their favor.

Decline set in, however, and by 1940 they numbered only around 200. Today only a handful remain, still running a store and holding services at the chapel in Loxwood. Older inhabitants of the area, however, can remember days when the lanes were full of carriages bringing the Cokelers to chapel, where they held meetings of praise and teaching, with hymns from their own handwritten book. Some remember also the signs and wonders of former days, especially the healing of the sick and, on one occasion, the raising of a dead man.

Perhaps the most revealing testimony to their way of life, however, is their custom of using as a prayer the seventeenth chapter of John—the high priestly prayer of Jesus—where he prays that his followers might be united in a deep oneness, "as I and my Father are one." This the Cokelers sought to put into practice in its purest and most uncompromising form—in a community lifestyle of the sort laid down in the Acts of the Apostles.

Chapter 10

The Twentieth Century

The whole subject of social justice, common living, and the sharing of possessions came to a head in the first quarter of the twentieth century with the rise of political communism. The followers of Marx, Engels, and Lenin, incensed at a society where the rich grew richer and the poor ever more wretched, saw the only answer as lying in the *enforcement* of equality through an uprising of the downtrodden proletariat to overthrow a comfortable bourgeoisie. All three had been atheists and were convinced that their sociopolitical reform would eventually render religion obsolete.

Yet it was soon apparent that such a system would run into the same insurmountable problems as the socialist utopias outlined in the previous chapter. There was no changed, regenerated heart, no common bond of humble service. Above all, no love. "Love" was not part of the Bolshevik vocabulary. While the Christian who lived with all things in common said out of love, "I have more than you, so I will share it with you," the communist said, out of frustration and revenge: "You have more than I, so I will seize it."

The Society of Brothers

The distinction is clear in the writings of a German named Eberhard Arnold. He had read the writings of the Hutterites[1] but could find no church which lived in that manner. So, fired by their vision, Arnold founded a Christian community at Sannerz in Central Germany in the early 1920s, calling it *Bruderhof* (lit., "brotherhood home" or "brotherhood farm"). Here possessions were held in common, worldly trappings shunned, and various industries started to provide a communal income. In 1927 Arnold wrote a pamphlet entitled "Why we live in community" in which he underlined the distinction between communist and Christian equality:

> With them, we stand side by side with the "have-nots," with the underprivileged, with the degraded and the oppressed. And yet we keep out of that kind of class struggle which wants to use loveless means against those who have injured the proletariat. . . . We take our stand in a purely spiritual fight on the side of those who fight for freedom, unity, peace among men, and social justice.[2]

The prerequisites were faith and love. Arnold went on to outline the nature of true Christian *koinonia:*

> Community life is like a martyrdom by fire: it means sacrificing daily all our strength and all our rights, sacrificing all the demands commonly made on life and assumed to be justified. In the symbol of a fire, the individual logs burn away so that, united, the flames send out warmth and light . . . into the land.
>
> When men voluntarily make a joint commitment to renounce everything that is self-willed, isolated or private, their alliances become signposts to the ultimate unity of all men, which is found in God's love, in the power of his kingdom . . . . We live in community because the Spirit of joy and love gives us such an urge to reach out to people that we want to be with them all the time. . . . We *have* to live in community, because God wants us in faith to give a clear answer to the unclear longings of people today.[3]

In 1930 Arnold discovered the existence of Hutterites in America and visited them. Pleased with what he saw, he became an elder of their church and affiliated his group with theirs. The rise of the Third Reich brought severe pressures from the secret police, so the community moved to Liechtenstein, then to England, then to Paraguay, before finally settling in America and England (New York, Connecticut, Pennsylvania, and Sussex).

Eberhard's son and successor, Heini, wrote a telling letter to an inquirer around 1950. He spoke of the heart that led the community's members into the life in common:

> We were tired of words, for they are cheap and can be heard almost anywhere; for who will say that he is against brotherhood and love? We wanted deeds, not words; we wanted bread, not stones.... We are here because we found that a "sensible and simple life"[4] was not enough, that Christ asks more of us than this. He wants the whole person.[5]

He went on to ask how one is to interpret such passages as 1 Cor. 12:25-26 or 2 Cor. 8:13-15 if not in a communitarian context. But he was careful to point out that the sharing of possessions is the outcome, not the foundation, of their faith:

> Full surrender to Christ means giving back everything that God has given us: our possessions, our talents, and our lives, to be controlled by God and his Spirit only.... Community of goods was and is the outcome of the love and grace that entered the hearts of those who were moved by the Spirit at Pentecost.[6]

The Hutterian Brethren (as they are now called) presently number over a thousand and live the way of life of the Western Hutterites. Visitors are expected to join in the daily work, which plays a central part in their life. As in the early monasteries, *laborare est orare*, to work is to pray. Working together in the woodwork factory or the sewing room is a spiritual blessing, as the communal meals, which Arnold called "consecrated festivals of community." Children are educated communally, and the goal of life is the laying aside of self-will. As Arnold said, Persons "with their present nature, without God, are incapable of community."[7] Only the "community-creating energy of God's Spirit" can make it possible.

The Jesus Family

Another compelling comparison between the communist and Christian ways may be seen in the story of the Ye-Su Chia-

Ting, the "Jesus Family" in communist China. While political pressure was forcing the China Inland Mission to cease operations in the land in the late 1940s, a group of Christians was living a life of quiet sharing at MaChuang in Shantung province. They owned 43 acres of land, shared among some 500 men, women, and children. Their diligent labors had led to a standard of hygiene, technology, and agriculture which far surpassed that of the surrounding communist collective farms. They shared as much as nine tenths of their produce with their poorer brethren in outlying villages. They carried out repair work on roads and bridges which the authorities allowed to fall into decay. Like the Hutterites, they cared even for those hostile to them in their hospital, because their medical standards were much higher than those of the secular world around them.

Nobody could be a leader in the Jesus Family unless he had obeyed the injunction of Jesus and had sold his house and distributed his wealth and possessions to the poor. One day, some visiting communists, asking to see the leader of the community, were nonplussed to see him pushing the dung cart. The communists, while claiming to have no leaders at all, organized everything by way of commissars, who had authority even over life and death and who exercised their powers with rigid severity.

The communist system had at its heart the weaknesses and corruptions of human nature. The sentiments were correct, but the heart of love and self-denial was missing. Medical supplies were stolen by nurses and agricultural produce by laborers. As a result, medical standards and agrarian policy were crumbling.

In contrast the Jesus Family demonstrated the qualities of heart which alone can make for true community: *love,* in that everything was readily shared with all; *integrity,* even to the point where a woman tied a note and some money to the leg of a stray hen which had laid an egg in the community compound; *self-denial,* whereby the whole community was prepared to go hungry in order to pay for one member to buy a ticket to Shanghai. Visiting communists were amazed that the large bunches of grapes on the community vines did not disappear overnight. They were also surprised that the pharmacy was always well stocked.

One European visitor, who stayed at MaChuang and wrote of his experiences, offered perhaps the most telling comparison between communist and Christian communalism. A young communist commissar from Tsinan, who had seen the capitalism and complacency of Christianity, boasted that it would be swept aside by communism all over the world. He was challenged to visit the Jesus Family. He did, and after a stay of some three days, appeared humbled and chastened. "I have seen," he said, "something which I did not know existed in the world. This is what we communists wanted to do, [but] we won't do it in a hundred years."[8]

Aiyetoro

In the mid-1940s a group of fishermen in Ondo Province, Nigeria, began to look for an alternative lifestyle. Weary of scraping their living from the sea and the marshland, and disillusioned with the idol worship of their tribes, they looked at the Jerusalem community of the Acts and saw in it a model. When an experience of the Holy Spirit came to them, they founded a communal village on the coast at the mouth of the Eruna Creek and called it Aiyetoro, which in the Yoruba language means "the world at peace." The church itself was named "The Church of the Holy Apostles." Its pastors, whom they named bishops, were Philip Eretan and Peter Jagbo. All members worked for the community—the men by fishing from dug-out canoes, the women by needlework and domestic duties. Many from the neighboring mission churches joined and within three years there were some 2,000 members.

Aiyetoro was carefully planned, with wooden causeways and

platforms to guard against mud in the wet season, and painted brightly in African fashion. It grew to the size of a small town. The community's industry brought sufficient income to purchase things virtually unknown for their day in the province: hurricane lamps, bicycles, a three-phase generating station, motor vehicles and sewing machines. A canal almost seven miles long was dug to aid transportation. The community did the work itself—the men digging, the women carrying away the earth in baskets on their heads. The whole enterprise took three dry seasons.

Members of Aiyetoro shave their heads as a sign of being different from the society around them. They wear a simple khaki uniform for work, produced in the community. But after the day's work (7:00 a.m. to 4:00 p.m.) each dresses in African fashion, the women with brightly colored head ties. Children are brought up communally and parents are urged not to be possessive. Once old enough, each is assigned to a craft or trade. These are fishing and net repairing, tailoring, carpentry, laundry, pattern-dying, and broadloom weaving. There are a doctor, a barber, and several nurses. Many who were formerly rejects in society are now well integrated in the community. One cripple was given work in the laundry and told a visitor that he was now happy for the first time in his life.

Services are frequently held in the chapel. They last two hours or so and contain much singing and charismatic ministry in the spiritual gifts. Everyday life is governed by a committee of sixteen elders. One of the elders, affectionately known as Baba (Daddy), presides and operates as a kind of estate manager. Each trade and craft has its overseer who takes charge of marketing its produce. Whatever the community does not use itself is sold. The aim is to be as self-supporting as possible. Members bring their individual or family needs to an appointed steward, and they are usually met. Meals are eaten together, since they constitute an important part of fellowship. Levels of health and literacy have been so improved in the community that they far outstrip those of the society around them.

In the early days, a few less laudable practices seem to have been retained from tribal custom. The senior bishop, known as Oba, was revered like a tribal king. Several older members kept two wives. Absence of more recent information prevents us knowing how Aiyetoro has dealt with this, but one visitor in 1957 stated that monogamy was being increasingly favored among the younger generation. And Oba, unlike so many of the semi-deified cult leaders of the day, did not live in luxury but joined in with the boatbuilding. The spirit of the community was expressed to a visitor by one of the elders, who spoke of the early days:

> The buildings you see are not of our own making but come from our God. We did not plan but were led by the Holy One of God who did it for us. Therefore those who did not give up their property for the common purpose have departed from us.[9]

The fruits of the community's existence are such that in the whole area round about, Aiyetoro has become a proverb for excellence.

The Present Situation

The period since the Second World War has witnessed far-reaching developments within the church. Evangelicalism, with its crusades and tent-meetings, has continued to rise. Alongside it the healing movement of the 1950s and the charismatic movement of the late 1960s are still active and influential. All have contributed to the health of Christianity. Evangelicalism has stressed the great truth of the individual meeting with God as the foundation of faith. The healing movement has presented Jesus as the Lord who still works signs and wonders and is compassionate to humankind. The charismatic movement has restored in part the use of the spiritual gifts and encouraged a fresh joy in worship.

But there have been problems. Healing has, in some circles, become an end in itself instead of being one of God's intended signposts to the gathered church. The charismatic movement also found it was not the magic wand some seemed to take it for. Many jumped on the bandwagon for as long as the joy lasted, but when the refining came, they quickly jumped off again. Many who were formerly aflame are no longer professing to be "baptized in the Spirit." All because they regarded the movement as an end rather than a means.

It is in light of this disillusionment that we must view the final editorial of Tom Smail, once editor of *Renewal* magazine and a leading figure in charismatic circles,[10] in which he spoke of his profound disappointment: elaborate claims had been unsubstantiated, prophecies remained unfulfilled.

Sadly enough, the evangelical movement itself has dealt the common life of brotherly sharing an unintentional blow. Its strength has been in the proclamation of the gospel, to the extent that more of the earth now knows the good news than at any point in its history. Conversions have been plentiful and genuine. Yet this very thrust has centered on the individual, seeking to lead the individual to Jesus as his or her "own, personal Savior." As a result, it has frequently overbalanced into an individualism and independence unthinkable in apostolic days. Selfish human nature instinctively likes the idea of a personal relationship with Jesus which allows one to live one's own private life exactly as one pleases. The notions of costly discipleship, sacrifice, being poor to the world, and sharing all things are too often overlooked amid zeal for the salvation of souls.

All this indicates the dangers of allowing one aspect of God's revelation to dominate at the expense of the rest. The new birth brings us into a oneness of knowing God. All alike are children and heirs. All are equal. This and the fullness of the Holy Spirit are intended to join Christians together into one body (1 Cor. 12:13).

Yet in this is a salutary warning to be heeded by the growing "community movement" itself: the same process could apply. If ever a community looked no further than itself, it would start to lose its way. It is a fruit, not a root. As Dietrich Bonhoeffer stressed,[11] mere love of community is not enough. Only a committed love for one's brothers and sisters can build Christian community.

The fruit of the movements detailed above has not, however, been wasted. Their impetus and blessing have been channeled into something new. The charismatic movement has been subsumed into most of the major denominations. It has also continued the "church in the home" principle through the house churches. Moreover, few churches do not now have some form of healing service. Mainstream evangelical church life has been strengthened by the charismatic movement. At the same time many trends and practices that were not long ago viewed with mistrust or scorn are today given a certain respectability. Today, many conferences have a charismatic flavor, with choruses, hands lifted in worship, delegates speaking quietly in tongues.

Unfortunately there has been a by-product of all this which has injured the sharing life of full community still further—the rise of celebration-style meetings.[12] Though not exactly new (Moody and Sankey were holding them in the 1870s), they have recently grown in popularity. They constitute a special-function Christianity, even sometimes a holiday Christianity. Chrisitans from all points of the spectrum can join together for a limited period to pray, share, worship, and even be entertained together, before returning to their normal daily lives.

This can provide a needed uplift for some, but its major drawback lies in the impression it conveys that Christian togetherness in any deep and committed form is an occasional, temporary affair. Christians can live their own individual lives with no attempt to share life in common, and receive an occasional "shot in the arm" at a convention, camp, or crusade.

Gone is the expectation that each local church and each individual practice a life of renunciation and active brotherly sharing *all* the time.

But over recent years voices have been raised in all denominations calling for commitment, community, and active discipleship. Books such as Michael Harper's *A New Way of Living,* Jim Wallis' *Agenda for Biblical People,* and Ronald Sider's *Rich Christians in an Age of Hunger* have been symptomatic of this change in emphasis. The following quotes reflect the growing consensus:

> The beginnings of a new society are coming into being. Those seeking this new way of life do not wish to impose that way upon others. Rather, by practical demonstration [they seek] to lead others freely to integrate themselves with it. They do not set out to reform society; they recognize that reformation must start with themselves and must spread outwards spontaneously. They do not seek to overthrow the present order; they believe that it is in the throes of its own mortal disease. They believe also that the values they stand for are the way of life and health and peace for men and for nations, and that these values can and must lived out here and now ... lived and not merely preached and planned.... They believe that fullness of life can be realized only in the act of giving, sharing, and serving; that getting, holding, and exploiting are the ways of death. The end of these ways is being demonstrated all around us today. Violence and self-seeking are taking on the form of a perverted religion and to it are being sacrificed the decencies and securities of life.[13]

> Our society needs more than a new perspective. It needs a new social vision. We can see the possibility of the church providing such a vision through its life. We can see the beginnings of a church living by biblical economics. It would be a real community in which competition was replaced by sharing.... The needs of the poor would take priority in the economic decisions and ministry of the congregation. Living at a fraction of present lifestyle levels would become a natural way of life as compassion takes root in the community. The presence of such a

people would be significant. They would be ordinary people who broke with the givens [the accepted norms] of their society. They would be concrete proof that it is possible to live a different way. [14]

Possessions are highly dangerous. They lead to a multitude of sins, including idolatry. Western Christians today desperately need to turn away from their covetous civilization's grasping materialism. [15]

The possession of wealth twists and distorts people's priorities and values and is a crucial obstacle in their sensitivity to God. [16]

Most Christians live in the world and go to church. God's intention is that we live in the church and go to the world. . . . The church must be a counterculture where Christians live together and share their lives together, where biblical values are not only taught but are lived out as a way of life. . . . There must be the corporate life and witness that very distinctively set us apart from the world as a people of God, called to renounce the world and its vain pursuits, and called to radical Christian discipleship under the lordship of Jesus Christ. . . . We *are* a counterculture. Our values are not the values of the culture around us. We do not embrace independence, but mutual submission and interdependence. We do not embrace privacy, but shared life, family, community. We do not embrace materialism, but Jesus Christ as owner and master over all we have and are. [17]

When Jesus says "You *cannot* serve God *and* Mammon," he is not just giving good advice. If Jesus is Lord, then Mammon is not. His people have no other gods. And all this becomes very practical. Our most important task is to demonstrate in the world to whom we belong. [18]

Amid gloomy predictions from sociologists and environmentalists, people at large are waking up to the fact that people are slowly destroying society by the selfishness of their own lifestyle. Voices are being raised in favor of devolution—smaller and more closely knit social groupings. The church also is taking a long, hard look at the issue of communal sharing. In every continent groups large and small are seeking to put it into practice. These vary in size from several hundred (for example, the People of Praise at South Bend, Indiana) to a handful of single people or an extended nuclear family, such as those listed by David Clark in his book *Basic Communities: Towards an Alternative Society,* or by Dave and Neta Jackson in their *Living Together in a World Falling Apart.*

When it comes to full sharing of possessions, the pattern remains as it has been in previous centuries. Some groups hold to the Jerusalem model with all things in common. Others adopt the Pauline stance of personal stewardship and contribution in case of need. Common to both, however, is a growing appreciation of the *covenant.*

Throughout Scripture God's call has always been: "I will be their God, and they shall be my people" (2 Cor. 6:16). As believers bind themselves together in a covenant of love, loyalty, service, and obedience in Christ, God will honor them. He has given his solemn word to do so. The result has been a growth in what we know as Covenant Communities—a term first coined by the Roman Catholics in America but given wider currency through the definition offered by Don Basham, editor of *New Wine:*

> A community of God's redeemed people, bound together in covenant love, submitting to compassionate authority . . . and manifesting peace, holiness, and family fidelity expressed through revered fatherhood, cherished womanhood, and motherhood with secure and obedient children. A community where loving correction and instruction produce healthy results in arts, crafts, trades, and commerce, providing prosperity and abundance for all its members. A community of faith, worship, praise, and selfless ministry, manifesting individually and corporately the gifts and fruit of the Holy Spirit. A community where all life is inspired and directed by the Spirit of Jesus Christ and is lived to his glory as a witness and testimony to the world. [19]

Whether or not these communities share a common purse, they constitute an attempt to regain the sense of the *common life* with its separation from the world, active love for one another, firm discipleship, and training in godliness. These have been . the motivation behind living churches throughout the centuries. Their proclamation is that God means what he says and that the early church pattern is a directive for all times.

Such communities will be a strong missionary witness by their life and example. There is much in the comparison drawn by some commentators[20] between Great Britain at present and the state of affairs in the sixth century. Then it was a pagan invasion of Angles and Saxons that had swept the land and driven Christianity to the fringes of the island, where it survived among the Celts. As had been shown, they were largely monastic and communitarian, but also vigorously evangelistic. Under the leadershp of such as Columba, bands of apostles spread over much of Britain, converting souls and presenting a new lifestyle of mutual love. Nor did it stop at these shores. Celtic missionaries also made forays on to the Continent, and for a time Iona and Ireland were the fulcrum of a spiritual renewal that was to reshape Britain—a renewal that had at its heart the full sharing of Christian love.

Today hedonism, humanism, and secularism have invaded and subdued the Western nations, forcing established Christianity to retreat until only pockets of genuine faith remain. Now there are fields ripe for harvest which beckon to these communities of faith to reap. The need is for true community, sharing, and material equality among the members of these groups, bred of love for Jesus and unity in the common cause. Then the world will indeed see, through a love lived out in practice, the beauty of the reconciling Jesus, as God again moves through the nations with bands of believers devoted to proving, in community, the risen triumph of the Lord Jesus Christ.

Chapter 11
Conclusion: The Characteristics of Christian Community

Amid the variety of applications, one recurrent principle emerges. In a climate where individualism is asserting itself strongly, groups of Christians are moved by the Holy Spirit to rediscover the life of unity and community. Sometimes this is conceived through a deep longing for close relationships and a common goal, sometimes through an open-minded reading of Scripture. Believers who read the accounts in Acts 2 and 4 and do not immediately reject them as obsolete can face the possibility that this might indeed be God's purpose for them. Their desire is to love God and each other (Mk. 12:28-31) and to reflect something of God's nature to the world about them (Rom. 8:29; Eph. 4:24). They find impressed upon their hearts the constant scriptural stress on God's call of a *people*—not just individuals. This awakens within them the desire to be together always, not just at church meetings.

Such is the basic impetus. But the question then arises: how is this common life to be structured? What ought a community to be and do? Many have realized with shock that the mere pooling of possessions, though apparently so costly a sacrifice, is not the recipe for instant success. The twelfth-century monastic reformer, Guerric of Igny, put it well:

> Many people have lived temperately and modestly in an abundance of worldly possessions and glory, while many also have behaved evilly whose garments were rougher and whose food more sparing.[1]

> I still want to impress upon you that truly blessed poverty of spirit is to be found more in humility of heart than in mere privation of everyday possessions, and consists more in the renunciation of pride than in mere contempt for property.[2]

Nor is the common life the panacea that some have wished it to be. Jean Vanier, founder of the l'Arche community, says it this way:

> Some people find it impossible to be alone. For them, [it] is a foretaste of death. So community can appear to be a marvellously welcoming and sharing place. But in another way, community is a terrible place. It is the place where our limitations and our egoism are revealed to us. When we begin to live full-time with others, we discover our poverty and our weakness, our inability to get on with people, our mental and emotional blocks ... our seemingly insatiable desires, our frustrations and jealousies, our hatred and our wish to destroy.[3]

Therefore it is essential that Christian community be *first* Christian, *then* community. The sole foundation must be Christ Jesus—devotion to him and obedience to his commandments. For the Godhead dwells in perfect community, and this corporate nature is powerfully implanted in those truly converted. Only this common bond, this common touch, this common reverence for one far greater than any human grouping, can build community securely. And this is alone inspired by the Holy Spirit.

The Marks of True Christian Community

1. Love—divine and human

Thus, a community must exhibit what we might call vertical and horizontal characteristics. Jesus summarized the commandments as a progression: "You shall love the Lord your God with all your heart, and with all your soul, and with all your mind, and with all your strength.... You shall love your neighbor as yourself" (Mark 12:30, 31). The vertical dimension must come first and issue into the horizontal. To have the one without the other is to fail. Much of Christendom holds to the first in varying degrees but knows little of the second.

Community people run the risk of basking in the second and neglecting the first. Each member must be born again, know the Holy Spirit, and have an active life of prayer, worship, and contemplation. Otherwise community becomes a social club. A regular, personal touch of God is necessary in order to have something to share with another. Where this does not happen, there is the constant danger of "the form ... without the power" (2 Tim. 3:5). Ideally the vertical and horizontal dimensions blend, as Aelred of Rievaulx found:

> Was it not a foretaste of heaven ... thus to soar aloft from the sweetness of brotherly love to the more sublime splendor of divine love; and now to mount the ladder of love right up to the embrace of Christ himself, now to descend it and repose pleasantly in the love of my brother?[4]

Dietrich Bonhoeffer presented his readers with a dichotomy: "Let him who cannot live alone beware of community; ... let him who is not in community beware of being alone."[5]

A recent writer has defined these terms in a useful way:

> Community is always poised between two poles: solitude and togetherness.... Solitude without togetherness deteriorates into loneliness. One needs strong roots in togetherness to be solitary rather than lonely when one is alone. Aloneness is neutral. Loneliness is aloneness cut off from togetherness. Solitude is aloneness supported by togetherness—"blessed solitude." Togetherness without solitude is not truly togetherness, but rather "side-by-sideness." To live merely side by side is alienation. We need ... to find ourselves in solitude before we can give ourselves to one another in true togetherness.[6]

2. Holiness

Without holiness, however, no one will see God (Heb. 12:14), let alone make a success of Christian community. The Lord Jesus who gathered his followers into a united, devoted, sharing band, also commanded them to "be perfect, as your heavenly father is perfect." The Greek here *(teleios)* suggests "having reached its end," "complete." Christians must give themselves to God for sanctification and not stop at justification. The aim is to be conformed more and more to the image of Christ. This process alone is the guarantee of progressive fruitfulness in community. God honors holiness. A community may be strongly evangelistic, witness to the inner city, care for the handicapped, or run a teaching ministry, but unless its members are each increasing qualitatively in godliness, there will be little fruit quantitatively.

3. Discipleship

Linked with this is the question of discipleship. It is a well-known issue in the church today since the publication of J. C. Ortiz' book *Disciple* (1975).[7] Basically, discipling operates in small groups. One member is acknowledged, because of his or her maturity in Christ, as leader. That leader then trains the others in the ways of God, sharing his or her own spiritual growth and experience. Here is a vital part of community. It is not the intention of sharing together merely to be nice to each other. If I have a secret sinfulness and a brother or sister discerns it, it *must* come into the open, lest it continue to damage both me and the community itself. Discipling strikes a blow at the prime enemy of community: self-will. In the bond of love each submits to the others to be trained, exhorted, and corrected. As long as all is done in a true spirit of love and with serving authority, discipling ensures the steady growth of each individual part.

4. Sharing

Sharing must be complete. Materially, *all things* must be in common, but it does not stop here. Religious orders are rediscovering today that sharing goes beyond goods. One's time, one's hopes and fears, one's motives, and one's desires—all must likewise be shared with brothers and sisters. In some respects, the sharing of possessions is easy: a quick, painful wrench, and it's done. Far deeper and harder is the sacrificial sharing of the deepest recesses of the heart.

5. Structure

No community can survive without structure. Jesus, in his parable of the wineskins (Matt. 9:17) was advocating a new structure. Many give the impression that Jesus was saying, "Away with the wineskin altogether!" His point was the opposite: lest the wine be spilled it *needs* to be kept in a wineskin—a new, supple wineskin. So we are not now free from all structures. Rather, we are to be reorganized along Christ's lines of discipline.

There is obviously a difficulty here, for several of the churches and groups listed in this book died of strangulation because they became overorganized. Jean Vanier comments: "Community begins in mystery and ends in administration. Leaders move away from people and into paper."[8] The fine balance can be achieved only through corporate wisdom in the Holy Spirit. Each has a gift, and many of these will be used in the community's structure. Helpers and administrators feature in the same list of ministries as prophets, teachers, and healers (1 Cor. 12:27-29). As the prophet and the teacher must ensure that they minister only and always in the Holy Spirit and not in their own strength, so too the helper and administrator. Financial, legal, and other domestic organizations will all then run smoothly under the hand of God.

6. Authority

There must be authority. The concept has so many connotations that human nature recoils from it and Christians often hold back in its application. Of course it must not be domineering. Jesus made that plain (Matt. 20:25-28). He modeled it by a life of constant humility, self-giving, and leadership by example. True Christian authority will have nothing of status or pride. It will correct with meekness, attempting to get alongside the brother or sister concerned in order to identify with them.

Yet authority must be strong and give a true lead. Proverbs 29:18 says, "Where there is no vision, the people perish" (KJV). It is up to the leaders to seek, find, present, and fulfill such a vision. As Jean Vanier commented at a recent conference on Christian community, there is a good deal of stress today on community as *mother*, with warmth, healing, compassion, nurture, and gentleness as her attributes. Far less attention is given to community today as *father*, with its connotations of authority, discipline, and direction.

7. Prophetic leadership

Leadership in community must be prophetic. God's people are to pass judgment on the spirit of the world with great strength. They are to be a fighting force in the midst of Babylon (i.e., the world), using all the spiritual power at their disposal. The spirit of prophecy is vital for the vigor and direction of a Christian community. "Where there is no prophecy the people cast off restraint" (Prov. 29:18). The prophetic word, intended primarily for the Lord's people, uncovers hearts and motivations (Jer. 6:27). This is indispensable for the proper growth of a community. It was the prophetic spirit in Peter that came so strongly against the deception of Ananias and Sapphira (Acts 5) and the self-seeking of Simon Magus (Acts 8). By it the church was cleansed. The same spirit of prophecy will come against the ills of a fallen church today. Prophets *named* the idols that had drawn away God's people. It was not as though the people had said: "From now on we'll forsake Jehovah and worship Baal alone." Rather they said, "Let us serve Jehovah *and* Baal."

The prophetic word names the idols (materialism, riches, selfish ambition, pleasure-seeking) and strongly demands their destruction. Such a word goes deep and provokes a strong reaction. Community people moving prophetically will be opposed with great vigor, but they will know the blessing of seeing these come and join whose hearts have been pierced and cleansed by the prophetic word.

8. Witness

A community must witness to Christ. The question is, how? Groups have attempted to answer it in a variety of ways and have failed. Some have been so given to evangelism that their inner life has been neglected and they have had nothing to bring converts to. Their hearts have wasted away amid much activity.

Others have sought to aid the poor, the aged, and the handicapped. Laudable though this may seem, and true to the compassion of Jesus, it has often ruined community by taking over. God becomes subordinated to people and holiness to social work. Churches waste their spiritual substance in anguished ministries to physical need. Of course the poor, the lame, and the blind are to receive the good news. Scripturally they will be the first to hear and follow. But this can only happen if the community is centered, not on those needing healing, but on the Lord, the Healer.

Nowadays it is fashionable in communities to be active politically as a witness to Christ. Civil rights marches, antiabortion rallies, the campaign for nuclear disarmament, etc., are popular causes. All attract throngs of Christian communities. Yet this, too, can be misguided and untrue to Scripture. Often this activity boils down to a frustrated attempt to reform the world apart from the radical repentance Jesus required of citizens of the kingdom of God.

This has never been God's intention. The world is in the throes of its own mortal disease. It is judged, fallen, in the grip of the evil one (1 John 5:18).

Jesus, in his prayer in John 17 refused to pray for the world

(v. 9). His followers are not of it (v. 16) even as he is not. They have been given to him out of it (v. 6) and will call others out of it. Peter, on the Day of Pentecost, did not say, "Go out and reform this crooked generation!" He said, "Save yourselves from it!" (Acts 2:40).

This follows the Old Testament types of Zion (the Lord's people) and Babylon (the world). The cry is: "Escape to Zion, you who dwell with the daughter of Babylon." (Zech. 2:7). The believer is to realize that Babylon is the enemy, bent on destruction. The church is to declare war on it (Jer. 51:34-35), and its end is destruction, as Revelation 17 and 18 show. Here again the cry is to separate from it (18:4). The Christians are meant to join together to form an *alternative society*, run along lines absolutely contrary to those of the world, passing judgment on the world and releasing its captives.

Any attempt, therefore, to reform the world is doomed from the outset, since it cannot receive the things of God (John 14:17), nor has it ever known him (17:25).

Reasons for Failure

In conclusion it would be valuable for any church seeking to share all things in common to piece together reasons for failure in earlier groups. So many have faded out after a generation or two, leaving a poor testimony. Yet the fault cannot be laid with the Lord who calls to community.

Following are some of the reasons for the dissolution of communities historically:

1. Loss of first love and first works (Rev. 2:4, 5)
This is the chief destroyer of Christian community and the primary tool of the devil, who attempts to sow lukewarmness, passivity, and laziness. The need here is for a heart response to Jesus, characterized by a diligent seeking of him, accompanied by a true love for one's brothers and sisters.

2. Overorganization

Overorganization quickly saps the flexibility of wineskins. Administration easily fills in as spirituality lapses.

3. Failure to oppose the flesh

Some communities have erred in being nice to people who turned out to be "wolves in sheep's clothing." A wishy-washy, human concept of "love" is at the heart of this failure to take seriously the community's responsibility to discipline.

4. Excessive writing

Some groups (e.g., the Labadists) felt duty-bound to answer in writing any criticism brought against them. So much spiritual and financial substance was lost in pamphlet warfare that decline set in.

5. Financial mismanagement

Sharing possessions brings equality and solvency, but income must continue. Some groups were so afraid of paid employment that they finally disbanded through bankruptcy.

6. Rejection of marriage

Some groups have so stressed the higher way of celibacy that they have not admitted married people. Some have even urged married persons to separate and have forbidden members to marry. While celibacy is indeed better and single people are more able to be devoted to the Lord (1 Cor. 7:32-34, 38), marriage is still to be held in honor (Heb. 13:4). To forbid it is a "doctrine of demons" (1 Tim. 4:3). Several groups (e.g., Cokelers) have dwindled away in numbers to the point of death for lack of children to form a new generation.

7. Worldly involvements

Some have become so engrossed in their attempt to reform the world that they lost their spiritual vitality. The Lord who is the source of community must also be the central ground of community life.

8. Lack of discipling and prophetic leadership

Communities have sometimes faltered and failed for lack of vision. Many communities found, on the death of the original leaders, no strength in depth to take their place. The prophet must train up another, as Elijah did Elisha. As Paul had his Timothy, his Epaphras, and his Titus, whom he had trained as a father, so must leaders of communities have those whom they are instructing and discipling for future leadership.

9. Excessive evangelism

Excessive evangelism can be detrimental to community life when it is pursued at the expense of personal spirituality and corporate relatedness.

10. Over-enclosedness

Some groups have so stressed being "not *of* the world" that they have overlooked that Jesus sends his followers out *into* the world in order to call people out of it (John 17:18). Enclosed monastic orders are not in the perfect will of God. In non-monastic communities, lack of evangelism has sometimes led to dissolution through lack of new members or to a dangerous degree of intermarrying between a few natural families.

11. Dissatisfaction

People in small community houses may want to be in larger ones, while those in larger community houses long for smaller ones. Everyone dreams of the perfect community and feels dissatisfied when they realize that their own is not so. Jean Vanier says it well:

I'd like to tell the many people in communities who are looking for the impossible ideal: "Stop looking for peace! Give yourselves where you are. Stop looking at yourselves. Look instead at your brothers and sisters in need. Be close to those God has given you in community today.... Everything will resolve itself through love."[9]

12. Pride in leaders

This is a big enemy in any church at any time. Often founders have become known as "Papa" and been revered almost as saints after their death. The danger of man-centeredness is constantly present.[10]

As the Holy Spirit is allowed full flow through a community, he will always show the true, narrow way, avoiding these pitfalls. A Christian community moving truly in the Spirit will prove, for as long as it "holds to the head" (see Col. 2:19), that the Lord honors communal sharing of all things in precisely the same way as in Jerusalem: "The word of God increased; and the number of the disciples multiplied greatly in Jerusalem" (Acts 6:7). "So the church . . . had peace and was built up; and walking in the fear of the Lord and in the comfort of the Holy Spirit it was multiplied (9:31).

Appendix

The research for this book was originally instigated by, and for the benefit of, the New Creation Christian Community centered at Bugbrooke, Northamptonshire, of which the writer is a member. In the course of study, however, it became apparent how little there is in print concerning community of goods and sharing in church history. So the scope of the work was broadened for a wider readership. Its intention is to fill the gap, to bring to attention the well-founded pedigree of communitarian groups, and to set within this context the New Creation Christian Community itself.

The roots of the New Creation Christian Community are Baptist. In 1969 the pastor and many of the congregation received a filling with the Holy Spirit at the time when the charismatic movement was spreading across the country. From that moment, the church sought to restore the New Testament pattern of life and government. Elders were appointed and spiritual gifts and ministries grew. In 1973 interest in Christian community was growing in many circles (cf. the number of books in the bibliography written at this time). That year an awareness came that the newfound oneness of heart in Jesus needed to find a deeper and more righteous expression in the sharing of all things—lives, time, hearts, and possessions. Hesitantly at first, but thereafter with growing confidence, members of the congregation moved into community houses and pooled their resources.

It worked. The Acts 2 and 4 pattern has proven effective even today. University graduates, doctors, and teachers found that Christ united them in love and sharing with converted dropouts, drug addicts, and gang members. Married couples and singles, old and young, discovered that community living brings a deep fulfillment in the Lord. At the time of this writing, some 650 people, from babies to 80-year-olds, live together in houses ranging from extended family dwellings on housing estates to a former hotel housing some eighty members, spread over an area from Nottingham to Milton Keynes.

Not everyone lives in community, however. Most do, but many others, who are as yet unable to live this way (because of age, unconverted spouses, inexperience in what is involved, etc.) are still covenanted and respected members of the church. The combined membership constitutes the Jesus Fellowship Church (Baptist).

The majority of members work outside the community, but there are several community businesses staffed by its own people, including a building and hauling company, a garage, a building supplies warehouse, and a chain of health and whole food shops, where, among other things, produce from the community's farm is sold. After working hours there are meetings for worship, Bible study, and evangelism. The community does not see itself as monastic. It is vigorously evangelistic, with teams of evangelists operating in several towns and cities in the Midlands. All members are encouraged and helped to find their ministry, where they will know fruitfulness in the Lord. Relaxation and leisure have an important place. Members are urged to cultivate their private devotional lives through regular prayer, Bible reading, and worship in the "secret place." Mealtimes are a focal point and are treated as important occasions of cementing relationships and enjoying togetherness in Christ.

The community has received from God the call to be "a city set upon a hill," visible to all around and demonstrating that God does indeed gather a people in oneness and lead them in the way of discipleship and fruitfulness. This has caused mixed reactions. Some have raised the age-old cry, "Extremists!" Some have confused the community with heretical cults, despite its statement of faith which sets out its orthodox and biblical position. Others are drawn to the light. Visitors are welcome and come in large numbers, either to the meetings or to stay in a community house for a few days. Sometimes other churches look to the community to help a particularly needy person. The community has, by God's grace, been able to help many such persons. An invitation is extended to Christians anywhere to spend the August bank-holiday weekend in the community, learning its vision and its lifestyle.

Some literature has been produced, including a definition of true Christian community. Based on that printed in *New Wine*, it gives an indication of the spirit, faith, and life of the hundreds who have been drawn to live this new and radical life of service, sharing, and obedience, whose motivation and goal is the Lord Jesus Christ:

> A *COMMUNITY* of people, born of God the Holy Spirit through repentance and faith in the Lord Jesus Christ; buried and raised with Christ in baptism; walking together in newness of life and witnessing to Christ's kingly power and rule.

> A *COMMUNITY* where each person is important and needed, having identity, personality and ministry; a community where all are united through God's covenant grace in lifelong commitment, functioning together as fellow-members of Christ's body, corporately displaying righteous oneness in the Holy Spirit.

> A *COMMUNITY* mutually submissive in Christ, where all are his ministers, and where leadership service is given in authority to uphold the holiness of God and to guard the flock of Christ, but always in humility and compassion, for the good of all; a community manifesting security and peace, where holy discipleship produces growth and maturity in Christ.

> A *COMMUNITY* in which holy manhood and fatherhood, holy womanhood and motherhood, are revered and family life is respected; a community where God's call to celibacy or marriage is recognized; a community where marriage sanctity is upheld and children brought up in godliness; a community

where infants are received in Christ's name and where the aged are esteemed and cared for in Christ's name.

A COMMUNITY-BROTHERHOOD displaying Christ's love in holy fellowship, where all race and class distinctions are abolished and a full sharing of wealth and possessions practiced; a community of a new heart and spirit where the righteousness of God is demonstrated, in the Holy Spirit's power, through a lifestyle of simplicity, integrity, purity, equality, and harmony; a community dedicated to excellence in crafts and commerce, and where disciplined, responsible people work together to provide prosperity, stability, and charity.

A COMMUNITY where Jesus Christ is Lord and where his divinity, virgin birth, atoning death, bodily resurrection, high-priestly ministry and coming reign are upheld; a community where the authority of the Bible as God's revealed Word is recognized; a society of worship, vision, faith, victory, and self-less service, manifesting the gifts and fruit of the Holy Spirit; a community where the Spirit of Christ gives direction and inspiration; a community "holding fast the word of life and shining as lights in the world"; a community bringing testimony and ministry to the world by showing Christ's power and the holiness of his church.[1]

Notes

Chapter 1

1. Especially the *Preaching of Peter* (early second century) and the *Ad Diognetum* (late second century).

2. 1 John 2:15-17; 5:19.

3. John 17, esp. vv. 6, 9, 15, 16; also 18:36.

4. Leonard Verduin, *Reformers and Stepchildren*, pp. 22, 23. London, Paternoster, 1964.

5. The writer heard these very proposals, advanced in all seriousness, at a recent conference on Christian community.

6. German *Gesellschaft* and *Gemeinschaft;* see Ferdinand Toennies, *Gemeinschaft und Gesellschaft*, 7th ed. Berlin, K. Curtius, 1926.

7. A more detailed examination is to be found in David Clark, *Liberation of the Church*, pp. 13ff. Birmingham, NACCCAN, 1984.

8. John 12:6; 13:29; Luke 8:1-3.

9. A. B. Kolb, ed., *Enchiridion, or Hand Book of the Christian Doctrine and Religion . . . by Dietrich Philip*, pp. 385ff. Alymer, Ont., Pathway Publ. Corp., 1966.

10. Aristophanes, *Ecclesiazusae*, tr. Benjamin B. Rogers, p. 89. London, G. Bell, 1902. Praxagora goes on to say how this is to be accomplished:

> I'll provide
> That the silver, and land, and whatever beside
> Each man shall possess, shall be common and free,
> One fund for the public; and out of it we
> Will feed and maintain you, like housekeepers true,
> Dispensing, and sparing, and caring for you.

Ibid., pp. 89, 91.

11. *Nichomean Ethics*, sec. Θ, 7, ed. Hippocrates G. Apostle, p. 147. Dordrecht, D. Reidel, 1975. Another proverb, which he does not cite, was *philōn ouden idion* ("among friends nothing is private").

12. Plato, *Republic* 4:464b; also 449c.

13. Virgil, *The Aeneid*, 8:327.

14. Virgil, *Georgics*, 1:126, 127; Ovid: *Metamorphoses*, 1:135.

15. Philo of Alexandria, *The Contemplative Life*, ed. David Winston, pp. 44, 45. London, S.P.C.K., 1981.

16. Cited in A. Dupont-Sommer (ed.), *The Essene Writings from Qumran*, p. 23. Oxford, Blackwell, 1961.

17. Ibid., p. 36.

18. Ibid., p. 37.

19. Ibid., pp. 76, 82, 83, 85.

Chapter 2

1. Another type, more commonly employed later in the Old Testament, is *Babylon*.

2. It should be noted that in Leviticus also (19:18), not long before the Jubilee section, we find the command to "love your neighbor as yourself," which Jesus encapsulated in his summary of the commandments.

3. Howard Kee, 1977, pp. 111, 112, sees similar implications in the miraculous feedings by Jesus: seek the Lord, and your material needs will be met.

4. The marginal rendering, "our bread for the morrow," is even closer to the sabbatical year position; c.f. Leviticus 25:20-21.

5. John H. Yoder, 1972, pp. 66, 67.

6. This was the more radical because the Israelites had long ceased to practice the Sabbath year and the Jubilee in any serious form. Creditors feared losing all, the nation found the freezing of credit intolerable, and the rabbis had even found an ingenious way round the issue, the *prosboul* (cf. J. H. Yoder, p. 67).

7. This is borne out of the following verse (v. 10), which is certainly pre-parousia.

8. Howard Kee, 1977, pp. 80, 81.

9. See chapter 5.

10. And, on occasions, to certain Gentiles, e.g., Matthew 15:21-28.

11. Kee, p. 152, sees a similar role in Mark 1:31, in the use of a Christian technical term, *diakonia* (service) and the imperfect tense, suggesting that Peter's mother-in-law was *in the habit* of ministering to Jesus' band.

12. We must not overlook the exhortation to love our enemies and to pray for our persecutors (Matt. 5:44), which Jesus calls an integral part of our being children of God. The love is of a different kind, with a different outworking. Love for enemies is the redemptive love of the cross, loving them in their sin and suffering for their sake. Christian love is the sharing love of the new kingdom society, loving one's sister and brother as oneself and enjoying equally the heavenly provision of God.

13. See chapter 4.

14. It would be misleading to belabor this point. "The earth," technically speaking, "is the Lord's and the fulness thereof" (Ps. 24:1). Paul was quick to refer to this principle (1 Cor. 10:26). Yet it was part of Satan's rebellion and sin to lay claim to what was God's. That same danger (with the same judgment) holds for humanity should it similarly seek to covet and appropriate the material things of life, which belong to God.

15. Peter Walpot, article 3 of *Great Article Book* of the Hutterites. For very similar modern declamations, see Jim Wallis: *Agenda for Biblical People* (New York, Harper and Row, 1976) and Ron Sider: *Rich Christians in an Age of Hunger* (Downer's Grove, Ill., InterVarsity Press, 1977).

Chapter 3

1. Another expression of this principle is found in Hebrews 13:13 (coming together to join Jesus *outside the camp*).

2. For example, the works early this century, of the German, Franz K. Meffert, who was admittedly attempting to discredit political communism.

3. In the Septuagint rendering of 3 Maccabees 4:6, *koinonia* is used for the sharing relationship of marriage.

4. Hal Miller, 1979, pp. 84, 85, cites the fourteen *ands* of Acts 2:42-47 as an indication that all the blessings were interrelated and inseparable parts of God's gift—signs and wonders, fear of God, prayer and worship, community of goods.

5. The word used for this donation is not *koinonia*, but *diakonia*, the usual word for "service," suggesting that this act of love was a matter of course.

6. For actual *meeting* in a house, other than residence, Paul uses a different expression, as in Romans 16:23, where Gaius is described as "host to the *whole church*" (of Corinth, from where Paul was writing).

7. In the Old Covenant, the Holy Spirit came only upon prophets, priests, and kings, or by special anointing.

Chapter 4

1. Clement of Rome, *Epistle to the Corinthians*, chap. 38, F.X. Glimm et al., eds., p. 39. *Fathers of the Church*, Washington, D.C., 1962.

2. Tatian, *Address to the Greeks*, chaps. 11, 32, A. Roberts and J. Donaldson, eds., pp. 16, 36. *Ante-Nicene Christian Library*, Edinburgh, T. and T. Clark, 1867.

3. Justin Martyr, *First Apology*, chap. 14, T. B. Falls, ed., p. 47. *Fathers of the Church*, New York, 1948.

4. *Epistle of Barnabas*, chap. 19, A. Roberts and J. Donaldson, eds., p. 132. *Writings of the Apostolic Fathers*, Edinburgh, T. and T. Clark, 1867.

5. Tertullian, *Apology*, pp. 99, 100, R. Arbesmann et al., eds., *Fathers of the Church*, New York, 1962.

6. Clement of Alexandria, *The Instructor* (or *Christ the Educator*), pp. 192, 193, S. Wood, ed., *Fathers of the Church*, New York, 1954.

7. *Mishnah*, Fourth Division, *Aboth*, 5:10, H. Danby, ed., p. 457. Oxford, Clarendon, 1933.

8. *Clementine Homilies*, 15:9, A. Roberts and J. Donaldson, eds., p. 240. *Ante-Nicene Christian Library* 17, Edinburgh, T. and T. Clark, 1870.

9. *Didache* (or *Teaching of the Twelve Apostles*), chap. 4. F.X. Glimm et al., eds., p. 174. *Fathers of the Church*, Washington, D.C., 1962.

10. Ibid., chap. 9 and Andreas Ehrenpreis, *Brotherly Community, the Highest Command of Love* (1650), ed. Society of Brothers, pp. 22, 23. Rifton, N.Y., 1978.

11. See below, p. 80.

12. Leonard Verduin, 1964, p. 17.

13. An example is the reverse of certain coins of the period, which bear the legend FEL. TEMP. REPARATIO (the restoration of happy days).

14. Arnobius, *Adversus Gentes*, 1:5, H. Bryce and H. Campbell, eds., p. 67. *Ante-Nicene Christian Library* 19, Edinburgh, T. and T. Clark, 1871.

15. Archelaus, *Disputation with Manes*, S. D. F. Salmond, ed., pp. 372, 373. *Ante-Nicene Christian Library* 20, Edinburgh, T. and T. Clark, 1871.

16. Augustine, *Sermons*, no. 355 (J. P. Migne's numeration in *Patrologiae Latinae*), cited in V. J. Bourke, 1964, p. 15.

17. John Chrysostom, *Homilies on the Acts of the Apostles*, pp. 161, 162. *Library of the Fathers* 33, Oxford, F. and J. Rivington, 1933.

18. Ibid., *Homilies on St. John*, chap. 19, T. A. Goggin, ed., pp. 191, 192; see also Homily 87, pp. 465, 468. *Fathers of the Church* 41, New York, 1960.

19. Job 22:18 in Septuagint version.

20. *Apostolical Constitutions*, 4:4, A. Roberts and J. Donaldson, eds., p. 109. *Ante-Nicene Christian Library* 17, Edinburgh, T. and T. clark, 1870.

Chapter 5

1. The community at Deir el Abiad, for example, numbered around 2,200. All pursued crafts and trades, and produce was exported as far as Alexandria.

2. Theodore, *Second Catechesis*, fragment. French translation, L. T. Lefort, ed., p. 38. *Corpus Scriptorum Christianorum Orientalium* 160 (Scriptores Coptici 24), Louvain, L. Durbecq, 1956.

3. Ibid., *Third Catechesis*, loc. cit., pp. 41, 50, 53.

4. *Sayings of the Desert Fathers*, B. Ward, ed., p. 5. Oxford, Mowbrays, 1975.

5. Ambrose of Milan, *De Nabuthae*, Latin text, C. Schenkl, ed., pp. 469, 470. *Corpus Scriptorum Ecclesiasticorum Latinorum*, 32, II. Vienna, F. Tempsky, 1897.

6. Augustine, Sermons, 355, 356, cited in Vernon J. Bourke, 1964, pp. 14, 15.

7. John Chrysostom, *Homilies on the Acts of the Apostles*, 7, p. 107. *Library of the Fathers* 33, Oxford, Parker, 1851.

8. Ibid., *Homilies on 1 Timothy*, 12, pp. 101, 102. *Library of the Fathers* 12, Oxford, Parker, 1843.

9. John Cassian, *Conferences*, 16:6, E. C. S. Gibson, ed., p. 452. *Nicene and Post-Nicene Fathers* 11, Oxford, Parker, 1984.

10. Augustine, *The Work of Monks*, R. J. Deferrari, ed., pp. 377, 378. *Fathers of the Church* 16, Washington, D.C., 1952.

11. Basil, *Letters*, A. C. Way, ed., no. 223 (pp. 127, 128). *Fathers of the Church* 28, Washington, D.C., 1955.

12. Ibid., *Ascetical Discourse*, M. Wagner, ed., p. 217. *Fathers of the Church* 9, Washington, D.C., 1962.

13. Ibid., *Long Rules*, M. Wagner, ed., loc. cit., pp. 249, 250.

14. Gregory of Nyssa, *On the Christian Mode of Life*, V. W. Callahan, ed., p. 151. *Fathers of the Church* 58, Washington, D.C., 1967.

15. Ibid., p. 146.

16. Julian Pomerius, *The Contemplative Life*, 2:9, M. J. Suelzer, ed., p. 72. *Ancient Christian Writers* 4, Westminster, Md., Newman Press, 1947.

17. Sozomenus, *A History of the Church*, lib. 6, ch. 31, English edition, p. 306. London, Bagster, 1846.

18. Paulinus of Nola, *Letters*, 34, P. G. Walsh, ed., p. 164. *Ancient Christian Writers* 36, Westminster, Md., Newman Press, 1967.

19. Cited by M. Villier, *Dictionnaire de Spiritualité*, xi: 1158. Paris, Beauchesne, 1948.

20. Benedict of Nursia, *Rule*, chaps. 33, 34. Edition used was *Households of God, the Rule of St. Benedict with Explanations*, D. Parry, ed., pp. 102-104. London, Darton, Longman and Todd, 1980.

21. "*Fifth Epistle of Clement*," from Latin text, fol. 76v°, *Divi Clementi Opera*, Paris, C. Guillard, 1544.

22. "*Epistle of Urban I*," A. Roberts and J. Donaldson, eds., Part 2, pp. 218, 220. *Ante-Nicene Christian Library* 9, Edinburgh, T. and T. Clark, 1869.

Chapter 6

1. Cited by M. Villier, *Dictionnaire de Spiritualité*, xi:1160. Paris, Beauchesne, 1948.

2. Ibid., loc. cit.

3. Aelred of Rievaulx, *Sermon on All Saints*, cited by C. Dumont, "Seeking God" in *Contemplative Community*, M. Basil Pennington, ed., pp. 124, 125. Kalamazoo, Mich., Cistercian Publications, 1972.

4. Ibid., p. 129.

5. In Latin, *nudi nudum Christum sequentes. Nudi* here suggests "naked," "poor," "without possessions." See Giovanni Gonnet: *Confessioni di fede*, p. 59. Torino, Editrice Claudiana, 1967.

6. E.g., inquisitors Alano, Peter Martyr, Salvo Burci, and "Pseudo-Reiner"; ibid., p. 83.

7. They were, for example, keen to oppose the errors of their contemporaries, the Cathars, who also practiced a degree of sharing of possessions but held a form of dualistic theology. See Jean Duvernoy: *Le Catharisme*, Toulouse, Privat, 1979.

8. "Credentes," "perfecti," "sandaliati," as opposed to "discipuli" or "amici."

9. Cited by Donald Durnbaugh, *The Believers' Church*, p. 46. New York, Macmillan, 1968; Scottdale, Pa., Herald Press, 1985.

10. Cited by J. Minter Morgan, *Enquiry*, 1827, p. 132n.

11. Cited by Walter H. G. Armytage, *Heavens Below*, p. 4. London, Routledge and Kegan Paul, 1961.

12. Albert Hyma, *Brethren of the Common Life*, pp. 65, 66. Grand Rapids, Mich., Eerdmans, 1950.

13. Cited in *Mennonite Quarterly Review*, 31 (1957), sec. 147; see also *Theologia Germanica*, chap. 51, J. Bernard, ed., pp. 214, 215. New York, Pantheon, 1949.

14. Howard Kaminsky, *Hussite Revolution*, p. 65. Berkeley, Calif., University of California Press, 1967.

15. Ibid., p. 285.

16. Carl J. Kautsky, *Communism in Central Europe*, p. 59. London, T. F. Unwin, 1897.

17. Ibid., p. 60.

18. Ibid., p. 75.

19. Joseph E. Hutton, *History of the Moravian Church*, second edition, p. 47. London, Moravian Publishing office, 1909.

20. Peter de B. Brock, *Political and Social Doctrines of the Unity of Czech Brethren*, p. 66. The Hague, Mouton, 1957.

21. Ibid., p. 80.

Chapter 7

1. *Die Aelteste Chronik der Hutterischen Brüder*, A. J. F. Zieglschmidt, ed., p. 42, Ithaca, N.Y., Cayuga Press, 1943.

2. Translation by J. Minter Morgan, *Enquiry*, 1827, pp. 145, 146. Other translations read rather differently. For example:

> Thus I do fully persuade myself that no equal and just distribution of things can be made, nor that perfect wealth shall ever be among men, unless this propriety be exiled and banished. But so long as it shall continue, so long shall remain among the most and best part of men the heavy and inevitable burden of poverty and wretchedness.

Utopia, London, J. M. Dent, 1951, p. 15.

3. Christian Neff and Robert Friedmann, "Community of Goods" in *Mennonite Encyclopedia*, 1:659. Scottdale, Pa., Mennonite Publishing House, 1955.

4. Ibid., pp. 658, 659.

5. Ibid., p. 659.

6. Georg Schnabel, *Defence and Refutation* (1538), in *Anabaptism in Outline*, W. Klaassen et al, eds., p. 237. Scottdale, Pa., Herald Press, 1981.

7. See above, p. 85.

8. More usually named Isenmann, or even Eisenmenger, he was active in Württemberg. His treatise is referred to by the Anabaptists, but I have been unable to trace it. Isenmann remains largely unknown, but Gustave Bossert wrote an article on him in *Blätter für Württembergische Kirchengeschichte*, n.s.5 (1901):141-158.

9. Cited by John Horsch, *Hutterian Brethren*, p. 132n. Cayley, Alberta, Macmillan Colony, 1974.

10. Ambrosius Spittelmaier, *Answers to a List of Questions* (1527), in *Every Need Supplied*, D. F. Durnbaugh, ed., p. 25. Philadelphia, Pa., Temple University Press, 1974.

11. Ibid., p. 25.

12. Ibid., p. 40.

13. *Anabaptism in Outline*, pp. 235, 236.

14. *Every Need Supplied*, p. 96.

15. Ibid., pp. 109-111.

16. Robert Friedmann, "A Notable Hutterite Document: 'Concerning True Surrender and Christian Community of Goods,' " sections 20, 28, 43, 137, 138. *Mennonite Quarterly Review*, 31(1957):22-62.

17. J. Horsch, *Hutterian Brethren*, pp. 131, 132.

18. *Archiv für Reformationsgeschichte*, 28 (1931):210.

19. J. Horsch, *Hutterian Brethren*, p. 131.

20. Ibid., p. 132n.

21. Ibid., p. 132.

22. Andreas Ehrenpreis, *Brotherly Community, the Highest Command of Love* (1650), pp. 18, 19. Rifton, N.Y., 1978.

23. *Every Need Supplied*, p. 67.

24. *Aelteste Chronik*, 1943, pp. 144, 145.

Chapter 8

1. Richard Baxter, *Gildas Salvianus*, p. 238. London, Robert White, 1657; also cited by J. Minter Morgan, *Enquiry*, 1827, p. 113n. Baxter's stance was, however, ambivalent. In a commendatory preface to a work by Thomas Gouge, subsequently printed at London in 1709, he anticipated by almost three centuries the current "prosperity" teaching: *Riches Increased by Giving to the Poor; or Mr. Gouge's Surest and Safest Way of Thriving.* No sense is visible here of voluntary poverty or common sharing. Rather, it is an altruism for profit: "Christian charity, rightly performed, is the surest way to plenty and abundance, it usually being rewarded with temporal benefits here, as well as with eternity hereafter." (p. 11)

2. Pieter C. Plockhoy (under pseudonym "Peter Cornelius"); *A Way Propounded*, letter 1. London, by the author, 1659.

3. Ibid., loc. cit.

4. *Every Need Supplied*, 1974, p. 145.

5. Two small communitarian enterprises are known early in the seventeenth century, particularly Nicholas Ferrar's society at Little Gidding. This was little more than an extended natural family living a quasi-monastic life, and they were decried as an "Arminian Nunnery" by staunch English Calvinists. Another was a religious industrial settlement in the Golden Valley in Wales, begun by Rowland Vaughan. Little is known of its history other than that it ceased to exist in 1620. Alun W. Owen: *Howell Harris and the*

Trevecka "Family," chap. 1, M.A. thesis, University of North Wales, Bangor, 1957.

6. Details in Paul Broutin, "L'oeuvre pastorale et spirituelle de Barthélemy Holzhauser," *Nouvelle Revue Théologique* (Louvain), 80 (1958): 510-525. For the nineteenth-century interest, see Jean-Pierre-Laurent Gaduel: *De la vie commune dans le clergé séculier,* Orleáns, A. Jacob, 1853.

7. Cited by M. Villier, *Dictionnaire de Spiritualite,* xi: 1165, Paris, Beauchesne, 1948. Laypersons were also involved in the community.

8. Trevor J. Saxby, *The Life and Ministry of Jean de Labadie, 1610-1674,* bibliography, part B. Ph.D. thesis, University of Oxford, 1984.

9. *William Penn's Journal of His Travels in Holland and Germany, in 1677,* p. 100. London, Darton and Harvey, 1835.

10. Ibid., loc. cit.

11. Gomer M. Roberts (ed.), *Selected Trevecka Letters,* p. 63, letter of January 19, 1756. Caernarvon, Calvinist Methodist Bookroom, 1956.

12. Morgan H. Jones, *Trevecka Letters,* p. 196. Caernarvon, Welsh Calvinist Methodist Church, 1932.

13. Alun W. Owen, *Howell Harris and the Trevecka "Family,"* 1957, p. 177.

14. Julius F. Sachse, *The German Sectarians of Pennsylvania,* 2:410. Facsimile reprint of 1900 edition, New York, AMS, 1971.

15. The best recent historian of the Amish, John A. Hostetler (see bibliography), was formerly Amish himself.

Chapter 9

1. Cited in an anonymous article, "Communism" in *Encyclopedia Britannica,* 11th ed., p. 701. Cambridge Univ. Press, 1910.

2. In the Greek sense of "household life" rather than the modern, financial application.

3. William A. Hinds, *American Communities,* 3rd ed., pp. 74, 75. Chicago, Charles Kerr, 1908.

4. John A. Bole, *The Harmony Society,* p. 38. Philadelphia, Americana Germanica, 1904.

5. Karl J. R. Arndt, *George Rapp's Harmony Society, 1785-1847,* pp. 227-233 (Philadelphia, Univ. of Pennsylvania Press, 1965) gives an account of a visit by a German duke.

6. George Rapp, *Thoughts on the Destiny of Man,* pp. 69, 70. (Ohio), Harmony Society, 1824.

7. My translation. German original in Bole, *Harmony Society,* pp. 43, 44.

8. Hinds, *American Communities,* pp. 109, 119.

9. Ibid., pp. 320, 321.

10. They pronounced "Amana" with the accent on the first syllable.

11. Richard T. Ely, "Amana, a Study in Religious Communism." *Harper's Monthly Magazine* 105 (1902), pp. 660, 661.

12. Ibid., p. 662.

13. Morris Hillquit, *History of Socialism in the United States*, p. 42. New York, Funk and Wagnalls Company, 1903.

14. *Memoir of the Late Anthony Norris Groves . . . by His Widow*, p. 267. London, James Nisbet, 1856.

15. Cited by Arthur Wallis, *Rain from Heaven*, pp. 83, 84. London, Hodder and Stoughton, 1979.

16. Cited by Roger Homan, "The Society of Dependents." *Sussex Archaeological Collections* 119 (1981), p. 201.

Chapter 10

1. See chapter 7.

2. Eberhard Arnold, *Why We Live in Community*, p. 4. Rifton, N.Y., Plough, 1976. Excerpts from the writings of Eberhard and Heini Arnold are copyrighted 1967, 1976, 1984 by the Plough Publishing House of the Woodcrest Service Committee, Inc., Rifton, NY 12471 and used by permission.

3. Ibid., pp. 5, 10.

4. Arnold quotes the terms used by his inquirer.

5. The letter is reproduced in *The Plough*, 3 (March 1984):2-4 and 4 (May 1984):13-15.

6. *The Plough*, 3:3, 4:15, 3:2, 3.

7. Eberhard Arnold, *Why We Live in Community*, p. 2.

8. D. Vaughan Rees, *The "Jesus Family" in Communist China*, p. 83. London, Paternoster, 1973.

9. "Aiyetoro," anonymous article in *Nigeria* 55 (1957), p. 373.

10. *Renewal* 82 (1979), editorial.

11. Dietrich Bonhoeffer, *Life Together*. London, SCM Press, 1954.

12. It has recently become fashionable to classify Christian meetings under three headings according to size: cell, congregation, and celebration.

13. Anonymous, "Community and the World Crisis," in *Community in Britain*, p. 13. London, Community Service Committee, 1940.

14. Jim Wallis, "Without a Vision the People Perish," in *Sojourners*, Vol. 9, No. 6 (June 1980), p. 6.

15. Ronald Sider, *Rich Christians in an Age of Hunger*, Downers Grove, Ill., InterVarsity Press, 1976, p. 112.

16. Jim Wallis, *Agenda for Biblical People*, New York, Harper and Row, 1976, p. 90.

17. Clay Ford in *Our Destiny Is Fellowship in Love*. Gloucester, Fellowship Press, 1977. p. 13.

18. A speaker at a conference on Christian community in Birmingham, 1980.

19. *New Wine*, February 1980, p. 30.

20. David Clark, *Liberation of the Church*, p. 157. Birmingham, NAC-CCAN, 1984.

Chapter 11

1. Guerric of Igny, *Fourth Sermon on John the Baptist*, 43:4, cited by M. Basil Pennington, "Together unto God" in *Contemplative Community*, M. Basil Pennington, ed., p. 154, n. 24. Kalamazoo, Mich., Cistercian Publications, 1972.

2. Ibid., *Sermon on All Saints*, 53:5, loc. cit., n. 25.

3. Jean Vanier, *Community and Growth*, p. 5. London, Darton, Longman and Todd, 1979.

4. Aelred of Rievaulx, cited by Charles Dumont, "Seeking God in Community According to St. Aelred" in *Contemplative Community*, 1972, p. 145. For Aelred, see also above, p. 89.

5. Dietrich Bonhoeffer, *Life Together*, pp. 57, 58. London, SCM, 1954.

6. David Steindel-Rast, "Contemplative Community" in *Contemplative Community*, 1972, p. 293.

7. Juan-Carlos Ortiz: *Disciple*, London, Lakeland, 1975.

8. From a lecture delivered at the Congress on Christian Community, July 1980, at Westhill College, Birmingham, U.K.

9. Jean Vanier, *Community and Growth*, 1979, pp. 23, 24.

10. CF. Gregory of Nyssa's words on the ministry of abbot, above, p. 82.

Appendix

1. This definition of community is taken from "The Faith and Life of the New Creation Christian Community." Northampton, Great Britain, New Creation Christian Community, 1981, p. 4.

Bibliography

(Anonymous)
1957 "Aiyetoro." *Nigeria*, 55:356-389.
1938 *Community in Britain*. London, Community Service Committee.
1942 *Community in a Changing World*. London, Community Service Committee.
1977 *Our Destiny Is Fellowship in Love* (extracts from newsletters of First Baptist Church, Chula Vista, California). Gloucester, England, Fellowship Press.

Amélineau, Emile
1889 "Histoire de S. Pakhôme et de ses communautés" *Annales du Musée Guimet*, 17. Paris, Leroux.

Armytage, Walter H. G.
1961 *Heavens Below. Utopian Experiments in England, 1650-1960*. London, Routledge and Kegan Paul.

Arndt, Karl J. R.
1965 *George Rapp's Harmony Society, 1785-1847*. Philadelphia, University of Pennsylvania Press.

Arnold, Eberhard
1972 *The Early Christians After the Death of the Apostles*. 2nd ed., Rifton, N.Y., Plough.
1976 *Why We Live in Community*. Rifton, N.Y., Plough.

Arnold, Heini and Annemarie
1974 *Living in Community, a Way to True Brotherhood*. Rifton, N.Y., Plough.

Babb, Laura L.
1975 "Iowa's Enduring Amana Colonies." *National Geographic*, 148:863-878.

Baldry, Harold C.
1965 *The Unity of Mankind in Greek Thought*. Cambridge, University Press.

Banks, Robert J.
1980 *Paul's Idea of Community*. Exeter, Paternoster.

Baumgartner, Ephrem
1909 "Der Kommunismus im Urchristentum." *Zeitschrift für katholische Theologie*, 33:625-645.

Bestor, Arthur E.
1950 *Backwoods Utopias; the Sectarian and Owenite Phases of Communitarian Socialism in America, 1663-1829*. Philadelphia, University of Pennsylvania Press.

Bigg, Charles (ed.)
1922 *The Doctrine of the Twelve Apostles* (Didache). London, S.P.C.K.

Bimeler, Joseph M.
1860 *Etwas fürs Herz! oder Geistliche Brosamen von des Herrn Tisch Gefallen*. Zoar, Ohio (no press).

Birch, Una
1909 *Anna van Schurman, Artist, Scholar, Saint*. London/N.Y., Longmans.

Bole, John A.
1904 *The Harmony Society.*
Philadelphia, Americana
Germanica.

Bonhoeffer, Dietrich
1954 *Life Together.* London, SCM
Press.

Bourke, Vernon J. (ed.)
1964 *The Essential Augustine.*
London, New English Library.

Broadbent, Edmund H.
1974 *The Pilgrim Church.* Paperback
ed., London, Pickering and In-
glis.

Brock, Peter de B.
1957 *The Political and Social Doctrines of the Unity of Czech
Brethren.* The Hague, Mouton.

Bruce, Frederick F.
1954 *Commentary on the Book of the
Acts.* London, Marshall, Morgan
and Scott.

Cerfaux, Lucien
1957 "La première communauté
chrétienne à Jérusalem" in
Recueil Lucien Cerfaux, 2:125-
156. Gembloux, J. Duculot.

Clark, David
1977 *Basic Communities; Towards an
Alternative Society.* London,
S.P.C.K.
1984a *Basic Christian Communities* (a
handlist). Birmingham, National
Centre for Christian Communities and Networks (NAC-
CCAN).
1984b *The Liberation of the Church.*
Birmingham, NACCCAN.

Clark, Stephen B.
1972 *Building Christian Communities.* Notre Dame, Ind., Ave
Maria.

Clasen, Claus-Peter
1972 *Anabaptism, a Social History,
1525-1618.* Ithaca, N.Y., Cornell
University Press.

Connor, Michael
1972 "The *De Instituto Christiano:*
Reflections on Contemplative
Community" in *Contemplative
Community,* M. Basil Pen-
nington, ed., pp. 47-60.
Kalamazoo, Mich., Cistercian
Publications.

Connor, Tarcisius
1972 "The Theology of Contemplative Community" in *Contemplative Community,* M. Basil
Pennington, ed., pp. 215-250.
Kalamazoo, Mich., Cistercian
Publications.

Desroche, Henri
1957 "Heavens on Earth."
Micromillénarismes et com-
munautarisme utopique en
Amérique du Nord du XVII e au
XXe siècle." *Archives de so-
ciologie des religions,* 4:57-92.

Duckworth, Edward H.
1951 "A Visit to the Apostles and the
Town of Aiyetoro." *Nigeria,*
36:287-340.

Dumont, Charles
1972 "Seeking God in Community
According to St. Aelred" in
Contemplative Community, M.
Basil Pennington, ed., pp. 115-
150. Kalamazoo, Mich.,
Cistercian Publications.

Dupont, Jacques
1967 "La communauté des biens aux
      premiers jours de l'église" in
      Dupont, Jacques: *Études sur les
      Actes des Apôtres*, pp. 503-519.
      Paris, Editions du Cerf.

Dupont-Sommer, André
1961 *The Essene Writings from
      Qumran* (tr. G. Vermés).
      Oxford, Basil Blackwell.

Durnbaugh, Donald F.
1968 *The Believers' Church. The
      History and Character of
      Radical Protestantism.* Scottdale,
      Pa: Herald Press. (1985 edition).

——————————————, ed.
1974 *Every Need Supplied. Mutual
      Aid and Christian Community
      in the Free Churches, 1525-
      1675.* Philadelphia, Temple
      University Press.

Ehrenpreis, Andreas
1978 *Brotherly Community, the
      Highest Command of Love.
      Two Anabaptist Documents of
      1650 and 1560.* Rifton, N.Y.,
      Plough.

Ely, Richard T.
1902 "Amana, a Study in Religious
      Communism." *Harper's
      Monthly Magazine*, 105:659-
      668.

Endenburg, Pieter J. T.
1937 *Koinoonia en gemeenschap van
      zaken bij de Grieken in den
      klassieken tijd.* Amsterdam, H. J.
      Paris.

Fogarty, Robert S.
1980 *Dictionary of American Com-
      munal and Utopian History.*
      Westport, Conn., Greenwood
      Press.

Frend, William H. C.
1952 *The Donatist Church.* Oxford,
      Clarendon Press.

Friedmann, Robert
1973 *The Theology of Anabaptism.*
      Scottdale, Pa., Herald Press.

Fülöp-Miller, René
1929 *Macht und Geheimnis der
      Jesuiten.* Berlin, T. Knaur.

Gilbert, Alan D.
1976 *Religion and Society in
      Industrial England . . . 1740-
      1914.* London, Longman.

Gish, Arthur G.
1979 *Living in Christian Community.*
      Scottdale, Pa., Herald Press.

Gonnet, Giovanni
1967 *Confessioni di fede, Valdesi
      prima della Riforma.* Torino,
      Editrice Claudiana.

Gross, Leonard
1980 *The Golden Years of the Hut-
      terites . . . 1565-1578.* Scottdale,
      Pa., Herald Press.

Grundmann, Herbert
1935 *Religiöse Bewegungen im Mitte-
      lalter.* Berlin, Emil Ebering.

Hardy, Dennis
1979 *Alternative Communities in
      Nineteenth Century England.*
      London, Longman.

Heide, Jan C. van der, et al., eds.
1976 *Labadisten yn Wiuwert. It
      Beaken*, 38, nos. 1, 2.
      Leeuwarden, Fryske Akademy.

Hillquit, Morris
1903 *History of Socialism in the
      United States.* New York, Funk
      and Wagnalls.

Hinds, William A.
1908 *American Communities and Cooperative Colonies.* 3d ed. Chicago, Charles H. Kerr.

Holloway, Mark
1951 *Heavens on Earth. Utopian Communities in America, 1680-1880.* London, Turnstile Press.

Holtzmann, Heinrich J.
1884 "Die Gütergemeinschaft der Apostelgeschichte" in *Straßburger Abhandlungen zur Philosophie, Eduard Zeller zu seinem 70. Geburtstage,* pp. 25-60. Freiburg i.B., Mohr.

Homan, Roger
1981 "The Society of Dependents; a Case Study in the Rise and Fall of Rural Peculiars." *Sussex Archaeological Collections,* 119:195-204.

Horsch, John
1974 *The Hutterian Brethren, 1528-1931.* Cayley, Alberta, Macmillan Colony.

Hostetler, John A.
1963 *Amish Society.* Baltimore, Md., Johns Hopkins University Press.
1974a *Hutterite Society.* Baltimore, Md., Johns Hopkins University Press.
1974b *Communitarian Societies.* New York, Holt, Rinehart & Winston.

Hutton, Joseph E.
1895 *A Short History of the Moravian Church.* London, Moravian Publishing Office.

Hyma, Albert
1950 *The Brethren of the Common Life.* Grand Rapids, Mich., Eerdmans.

Jackson, Dave and Neta
1972 *Living Together in a World Falling Apart.* Carol Stream, Ill., Creation House.

Jackson, Frederick J. F. and Lake, Kirsopp
1920, 1933 *The Beginnings of Christianity,* vols. 1, 4. London/New York, Macmillan.

Jones, Morgan H.
1932 "The Religious-Industrial Community at Trevecka" in Jones, M.H.: *The Trevecka Letters,* pp. 185-206. Caernarvon, Wels Calvinist Methodist Church.

Kaminsky, Howard
1967 *A History of the Hussite Revolution.* Berkeley, Calif., Universit of California Press.

Kautsky, Carl J.
1897 *Communism in Central Europe at the Time of the Reformation* (tr. J. F. and E. G. Mulliken). London, T. F. Unwin.

Kee, Howard, C.
1977 *Community of the New Age. Studies in Mark's Gospel.* London, SCM Press.

Klaassen, Walter, (ed.)
1981 *Anabaptism in Outline. Selecte Primary Sources.* Scottdale, Pa. Herald Press.

Littell, Franklin H.
1964 *The Origins of Sectarian Protestantism.* London/New York, Macmillan.

McAndrew, Donald
1942 "The Sussex Cokelers, a Curiou Sect." *Sussex County Magazin* 16:346-350.

McDonnell, Ernest W.
1954 *The Beguines and Beghards in Medieval Culture.* New Brunswick, N.Y., Rutgers University Press.

Martin, Francis
1972 "Monastic Community and the Summary Statements in Acts" in *Contemplative Community,* M. Basil Pennington, ed., pp. 13-46. Kalamazoo, Mich., Cistercian Publications.

Miller, Hal
1979 *Christian Community, Biblical or Optional?* Ann Arbor, Mich., Servant Publications.

Mörner, Magnus
1953 *The Political and Economic Activities of the Jesuits in the La Plata Region* (tr. A. Read). Stockholm, Library and Institute of Ibero-American Studies.

Montgomery, John M.
1962 *Abodes of Love.* London, Putnam.

Morgan, J. Minter
1827 *An Enquiry Respecting Private Property and the Authority and Perpetuity of the Apostolic Injunction to a Community of Goods.* Appended to 1850 ed. of Morgan's *The Christian Commonwealth.* London, C. Gilpin.

Müller, Lydia
1927 *Der Kommunismus der mährischen Wiedertäufer.* Leipzig, M. Heinsius. Also as *Schriften des Vereins für Reformationsgeschichte 45, no.1.*

Muston, Alexis
1978 *Israel of the Alps: a Complete History of the Vaudois of Piedmont and Their Colonies* (tr. J. Montgomery). Facsimile reprint of 1857 Glasgow ed. New York, AMS Press.

Neff, Christian
1969 "Community of Goods" in *Mennonite Encyclopedia,* 1:658-662. Scottdale, Pa., Mennonite Publishing House.

Nordhoff, Charles
1875 *The Communistic Societies of the United States.* London, J. Murray.

Owen, Alun W.
1957 *A Study of Howell Harris and the Trevecka "Family,"* 1752-1760. M.A. thesis, University of North Wales, Bangor.

Palmer, Parker J.
1977 *A Place Called Community.* Wallingford, Pa., Pendle Hill Publications (Pendle Hill Pamphlet no. 212).

Pennington, M. Basil
1972 "Together unto God: Contemplative Community in the Sermons of Guerric of Igny" in *Contemplative Community,* M. Basil Pennington, ed., pp. 151-170. Kalamazoo, Mich., Cistercian Publications.

Perkins, William R.
1891 *History of the Amana Society.* Iowa City, The University.

Plockhoy, Pieter C. (under pseudonym Cornelius, Peter)
1659a *A Way Propounded to Make the Poor in These and Other Nations Happy.* London (no press).
1659b *An Invitation to the Aforementioned Society, Showing the Excellence of the True Christian Love.* (London (no press).

Pöhlmann, Robert von
1893, 1901 *Geschichte des antiken Kommunismus und Sozialismus.* München, Beck.

Popkes, Wiard
1975, 76 "Gemeinschaft" in *Reallexicon für Antike und Christentum,* 71/72:1100-1145. Stuttgart, A. Hiersemann.

Pusey, Edward B., et al., eds.
1838-85 *A Library of the Fathers of the Holy Catholic Church.* Oxford, J. H. Parker.

Quasten, Johannes, ed.
1946-67 *Ancient Christian Writers.* Westminster, Md., Newman Press.

Randall, Emilius O.
1899 *History of the Zoar Society; a Sociological Study in Communism.* Columbus, Ohio, A. H. Smythe.

Rapp, J. George
1824 *Thoughts on the Destiny of Man.* (No place or press)

Rees, D. Vaughan
1973 *The "Jesus Family" in Communist China.* Paperback ed., London, Paternoster.

Rexroth, Kenneth
1975 *Communalism, from Its Origins to the Twentieth Century.* London, Owen.

Rideman (Riedemann), Peter
1970 *Confession of Faith; an Account of Our Religion, Doctrine, and Faith.* Rifton, N.Y., Plough.

Roberts, Alexander, and Donaldson, James, eds.
1867-97 *Ante-Nicene Christian Library.* Edinburgh, T. and T. Clark.

Runzo, Jean
1980 "Hutterite Communal Discipline, 1529-1565." *Archiv für Reformationsgeschichte,* 71:16-179.

Scheuner, Gottlieb
1884 *Inspirations-Historie.* (Chronicle of the Amana Society). Amana, Iowa (no press).

Schilling, Otto
1908 *Reichtum und Eigentum in der altkirchlichen Literatur.* Freiburg i.B., Herder.

Schopp, Ludwig, et al., eds.
1947- *Fathers of the Church.* Washington, D.C., Catholic University of America Press.

Schubert, Hans von
1919 "Der Kommunismus der Wiedertäufer in Münster and seine Quellen." *Sitzungsberichte der Heidelberger Akademie,* 11:1-58.

Schwalm, Marie-Benoît
1906 "Communisme" in *Dictionnaire de théologie catholique,* fasc. 1, 574-596. Paris, Letouzey and Ané.

Sessler, Jacob J.
1933 *Communal Pietism Among Early American Moravians.* N. York, Holt.

Spangenberg, August G.
1838 *The Life of Nicholas Lewis,
       Count Zinzendorf* (tr. S.
       Jackson). London, S.
       Holdsworth.

Taylor, R. Bruce
1910a "Communism" in
       *Encyclopaedia of Religion and
       Ethics*, 3:776-780.
1910b "Communistic Societies of
       America" in *ibid.*, 3:780-787.
       Edinburgh, T. and T. Clark.

Tillard, Jean-Marie-Roger
1975 "Comunità" in *Dizionario degli
       Istituti di Perfezione*, 2:1366-
       1376. Roma, Edizioni Paoline.

Uttendörfer, Otto
1925 *Wirtschaftsgeschichte und Reli-
       gionssoziologie Herrnhuts*. Herrn-
       hut, Missionsbuchhandlung.
1926 *Wirtschaftsgeist und Wirts-
       chaftsorganisation Herrnhuts*.
       Herrnhut, Missionsbuchhand-
       lung.
1940 *Zinzendorfs christliches Le-
       bensideal*. Gnadau,
       Unitätsbuchhandlung.

Vanier, Jean
1979 *Community and Growth*.
       London, Darton, Longman and
       Todd.

Verduin, Leonard
1964 *The Reformers and Their Step-
       children*. London, Paternoster.

Vermès, Geza
1977 *The Dead Sea Scrolls; Qumran
       in Perspective*. London, Collins.

Villier, Marcel
1948 "Communautaire, Vie" in *Dic-
       tionnaire de Spiritualité*, fasc.
       11:1156-1184. Paris.
       Beauchesne.

Wallis, Arthur
1979 *Rain from Heaven* (formerly *In
       the Day of Thy Power*). London,
       Hodder.

Wallis, Jim
1976 *Agenda for Biblical People*. New
       York, Harper and Row.

Walpot, Peter
1957 "Concerning True Surrender
       and Christian Community of
       Goods." (Hutterite text of 1577).
       Mennonite Quarterly Review,
       31:22-62.

Ward, Benedicta
1975 *The Sayings of the Desert
       Fathers*. Oxford, Mowbrays.

Webber, Everett
1959 *Escape to Utopia; the Com-
       munal Movement in America*.
       New York, Hastings House.

Winterton, Earl
1931 "The Cokelers, a Sussex Sect."
       Sussex County Magazine, 5:717-
       722.

Workman, Herbert B.
1913 *The Evolution of the Monastic
       Ideal*. London, C. H. Kelly.

Yoder, John H.
1972 *The Politics of Jesus*. Grand
       Rapids, Mich., Eerdmans.

In addition, useful material may be
found in the following current
magazines:

Coming Together
published by Fellowship of Hope,
414 W. Wolf,
Elkhart, IN 46516.

Community
    published by National Centre for
    Christian Communities and
    Networks,
    Westhill College, Weoley Park Road,
    Selly Oak,
    Birmingham B29 6LL.

Grassroots
    (formerly *Towards Renewal*),
    published by Post Green
    Community,
    57 Dorchester Road,
    Lytchett Minster,
    Poole, Dorset BH16 6JE.

Newness
    occasional publication of New
    Creation Christian Community,
    New Creation Farm,
    Nether Heyford,
    Northants, NN7 3LB.

The Plough
    published by Hutterian Society of
    Brothers,
    Woodcrest Bruderhof,
    Rifton, NY 12471
    (for British market c/o Darvell
    Bruderhof,
    Robertsbridge,
    E. Sussex TN32 5DR)

Soujourners
    published at 1309 L. Street NW,
    Washington, DC 20005.

Scripture Index

Old Testament

Genesis

Exodus

Leviticus

Deuteronomy

Joshua

1 Samuel

Nehemiah

Job

Psalms

Proverbs

Song of Solomon

Isaiah

Jeremiah

Hosea

Amos

Zechariah

Apocrypha

3 Maccabees

New Testament

Matthew

Mark

Luke

General Index

The Author

Trevor John Saxby was born at Epsom, Surrey, England, in 1954. While at Kings College School, Wimbledon, he began to look at monastic and alternative lifestyles as a result of his study and of his own search for a faith.

From 1972 to 1976 he studied German and French at St. Edmund Hall, Oxford, graduating with an honors degree and a distinction in German. During his first year at Oxford, he also found a living Christian faith. In his final year he made contact with the Jesus Fellowship Church (Baptist) at Bugbrooke, Northamptonshire, a group which was seeking to rediscover the practice of community of goods as outlined in the Acts of the Apostles. He became a member there in 1976.

Having trained as a teacher of modern languages, Saxby has worked at a number of comprehensive schools in the Midlands of England. In 1979 he returned to Oxford for doctoral research on Christian community of goods. In 1984 he was awarded a Ph.D. degree in theology, was a thesis on the life and witness of the Labadists, a seventeenth-century Dutch community with an offshoot in Maryland.

In 1980 Trevor Saxby married Angela J. May. He is presently employed by Northamptonshire County in a comprehensive school, where he teaches German and French. He is also actively involved in pastoral and evangelistic work for the Jesus Fellowship. He lives in the community's largest house, a former hotel called Cornhill Manor at Pattishall in Northamptonshire, England.